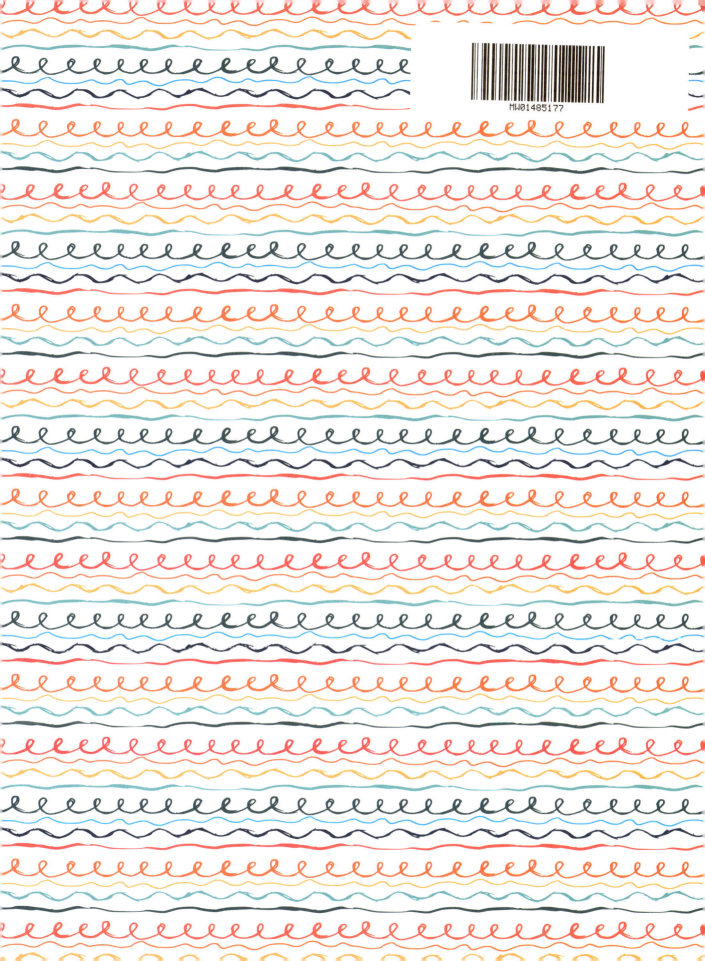

Jane Kim Nicholson's book, *More Please! Food Kids Love,* is a loving dialogue about how we can feed our children with Jane's "simple is best" approach. The book balances health, taste, and simplicity in every recipe while celebrating diversity in an accessible, child-friendly way. No culinary degree is needed here — just a love for your children and a desire for their well-being. Whether you're looking for unique (out of the) lunchbox ideas, quick weeknight dinners, or a special weekend treat, Jane guides you with an easy-to-follow approach. Her meals are practical, nutritious, and — above all — delicious. Beyond the fun meals you'll make for your family, *More Please! Food Kids Love* encourages a nurturing meal environment that strengthens the family bond. These aren't just recipes; they're catalysts for conversation, shared moments, and a broader understanding of the world.

—Agnes Hsu, AUTHOR AND FOUNDER OF WWW.HELLOWONDERFUL.CO

This is a superb cookbook, of course, and the ideas and creativity and care are obvious on every page. But it's more than another cookbook — it is a love letter to a Korean heritage, living in America, and the beauty and vitality that come from embracing such diversity. This is a book for everyone, a book that demonstrates both how to be proud of where we are from and also how to move forward and embrace new ideas and cultures as well — and the food and recipes are delicious!

— David C. Kang, MARIA CRUTCHER PROFESSOR OF INTERNATIONAL RELATIONS AT THE UNIVERSITY OF SOUTHERN CALIFORNIA AND DIRECTOR OF THE USC KOREAN STUDIES INSTITUTE

More Please! Food Kids Love is a game-changer for busy parents like me. Its collection of easy, healthy recipes and lunchbox ideas will transform any mealtime in your household. What makes this cookbook truly special is the nostalgic twist it brings to the table, reminding us of our own cherished childhood memories around food. As an Asian American, I am happy to see the inclusion of a variety of delicious Asian recipes that instill in our children a love for diverse flavours. This cookbook will strike a chord with many, making it an essential addition to any family kitchen!

— Joan Nguyen, CO-FOUNDER OF BÜMO

To know Jane is to love her, and this book is SO HER. Her family-friendly recipes (some with a Korean twist) are full of colour, nourishing ingredients, and love. We are obsessed with how simple and approachable everything is! Your kiddos will for sure be saying "MORE PLEASE!"

— Kelly Pfeiffer, @EATTHERAINBOW_KIDS AND AUTHOR OF *SUPERFOOD WEEKNIGHT MEALS*

Jane and her family have been our friends for years, and our sons are of a similar age, which is why this book resonates with us in many ways. We cannot recommend this cookbook enough! Its thoughtful details, creative ideas, and easy-to-follow recipes will make your meal planning a breeze. From weeknight dinners to special occasions, this cookbook has become an essential part of our kitchen — even our five-year-old loves to join in. Don't miss out on this gem — grab a copy and get ready to witness the positive impact it'll have on your family's cooking experience. Trust us, it's an absolute must-have!

— John Stamos and Caitlin McHugh Stamos

Just a friendly reminder that the recipes in this cookbook can be adjusted to match your child's age and stage of growth. We want to make sure every bite is a safe and enjoyable experience! For kids under the age of five, we need to be extra careful about choking hazards. So, let's get creative and slice, dice, and shape our foods into appropriate sizes and textures for kids. For personalized tips and tricks on age-appropriate recipes and keeping those taste buds happy and safe, don't hesitate to reach out to your pediatrician or a registered dietitian. Happy cooking, and let the delicious adventures begin!

For lunchbox safety tips, turn to page 180.

PLUMLEAF PRESS

www.plumleafpress.com

@plumleafbooks plumleafpress plumleafpress

Photography and food styling on recipe pages by Jane Kim Nicholson.

23 24 25 26 27   5 4 3 2 1

ISBN 978-1-7782428-6-1

Printed in China

MORE, PLEASE!

FOOD KIDS LOVE

MORE, PLEASE!

FOOD KIDS LOVE

JANE KIM NICHOLSON

CREATOR OF @FOOD.KIDS.LOVE

PLUMLEAF PRESS

DEDICATION

This book is dedicated to my husband, Mark, and our two amazing kids, Ella and Chase, whose support and endless taste testing made it all possible.

CONTENTS

FOREWORD

In the world of parenting, there are few endeavours more rewarding and simultaneously challenging than nourishing our children. As parents, we strive to provide them with not only the essential nutrients their bodies require but also the joy, love, and cultural connections that food can bring. We understand that food is more than just something we eat; it is a reflection of our heritage, traditions, and cherished memories. It is with this deep appreciation for the power of food that we are delighted to introduce you to *More, Please! Food Kids Love*.

In *More, Please! Food Kids Love*, Jane Kim Nicholson invites us to learn through her own experiences, sharing her passion for celebrating and embracing cultural diversity in cuisine with practical everyday guidance. With a genuine love for food instilled by her Korean immigrant parents, Jane's kitchen has become a place where simplicity, balance, health, and taste converge.

Jane's philosophy is refreshingly uncomplicated: "Simple is best." She empowers parents with creative and accessible ideas to make tasty, nutritious meals that not only please the little ones but also satisfy the discerning palates of adults. Through her blog and popular Instagram account @Food.Kids.Love, Jane has already inspired countless families with her everyday suggestions for both nutritious and delicious kid-friendly meals.

Jane builds on her knowledge and experience in *More, Please! Food Kids Love* to provide you with nearly 100 recipes. You'll find plenty of meal ideas, from breakfast to dinner, with lunches, snacks, and themed treats in between. Moreover, Jane's Korean heritage shines through, enriching the collection with an Asian influence and a section dedicated to the Asian Pantry.

But this book is more than a compilation of delectable recipes. Jane understands the daily challenges of busy parents and offers practical tips on crafting attractive and nutritious lunchboxes that will make your kid's school-lunch packing a breeze. She even encourages your little ones to join in the cooking process, fostering their love for food and expanding their palates.

As you turn the pages of *More, Please! Food Kids Love*, you'll sense the love and passion Jane pours into every dish. Some of her recipes, passed down through generations and infused with her own creative twists, are a testament to the enduring power of food to connect us to our heritage and create lasting memories.

Whether you are seeking inspiration to tackle hectic mornings, solve dinnertime dilemmas, or surprise your loved ones with fun holiday treats, this book has you covered. Jane's collection celebrates vibrant global flavours and embraces cultural diversity, and is a reflection of her own heritage and the values she imparts to her multiracial children.

So, prepare to embark on a culinary journey that marries simplicity, nutrition, and a celebration of cultural diversity. Let *More, Please! Food Kids Love* be your trusted companion, guiding you to create meals and snacks that will leave your kiddo — and the entire family — eagerly asking for "More, Please!" Embrace the joy of feeding your children, nourishing their bodies and spirits, and building a lifelong love affair with food.

Happy cooking, happy eating, and may your family's table overflow with love and laughter!

— Dani Lebovitz, also known as Kid Food Explorers, and Alicia "Chacha" Miller, known as The Cardamom, Registered Pediatric Dietitian Nutritionists

Photo by Katie Blauser

We have dedicated our careers to promoting diversity, equity, and inclusion in our approach to food and nutrition education. Our mission is to contribute to the growth of a healthier generation by providing accessible and easy-to-understand resources that inspire, guide, and empower parents to nourish their families with joy, love, connection, and nutrition. We are passionate about fostering confident kids who develop a healthy relationship with all foods and their growing bodies. And when it comes to feeding our little ones, we understand the importance of practical and sustainable routines that seamlessly integrate into the family structure.

Dani and Chacha

INTRODUCTION

When I was growing up, I had no idea that the piping hot spicy dish my mother made was different from what my friends' mothers made. It never occurred to me that it smelled different, looked different, and that other people might think it was foreign or strange. To me, it was just kimchi cooked in a bubbling stew with hot pepper paste and spicy pork. The aroma was my mother. It was my home. And now, it is my childhood.

As I became older and entered my teenage years, I remember yelling at my mother to close my bedroom door so that my clothes wouldn't smell like the food she cooked. I remember asking for plain bologna sandwiches on white bread, and other times, throwing my lunches in the garbage can when nobody was looking.

And now, things have come full circle. When my mother comes to visit me in Los Angeles, the very same dish that had me closing my bedroom door is the very first thing that I request. It's the one dish I always crave and the only dish that no one can compete with because my mother makes it best.

I am a daughter of hardworking Korean immigrant parents. Most of my strongest memories are triggered from the scents of my mother's cooking. It was at home that I built up a genuine love of food. I also gained a lot of my knowledge and experience from helping in my parents' restaurants and cafes growing up. Little did I know that those skills would transfer into my own kitchen one day, where I would spend most of my days developing and testing recipes, with my two little taste-testers acting as my toughest judges.

My whole approach to cooking and feeding my children is this: simple is best — without sacrificing balance, health, and taste, of course. I have come to realize that creating tasty and nutritious meals for kids doesn't have to be complicated. And with less pressure, and with simple, healthier swaps and add-ins, paired with creative displays, you can feed your kids and your entire family food they love to eat.

As you browse through the pages of this book, you will see that it is an extension of my blog, Food Kids Love, and Instagram account @food.kids.love — non-judgmental, accessible spaces that provide everyday inspiration for kid-friendly snacks and lunches. This cookbook includes breakfast, lunch, dinner, and snack ideas as well as recipes inspired by Asian cooking. As much as this book is about inspiring you to make simple, healthy, kid-friendly meals, it's also about celebrating and embracing cultural diversity.

In recognition of my past and my children's present and future, I present to you recipes that feel close to home. Many are recipes that have been passed down to me to which I have added my own twists, recipes that I hope, one day, my children will be making for their own children — all while being super kid-friendly.

If your kids are willing and wanting to help, start with small age-appropriate tasks. For little ones, just let them play in a big sensory bin with measuring cups and spoons, and let them watch as you work. As my daughter got older, she wanted to get more involved in the cooking process and, with this constant exposure, she became more confident in the kitchen — and open to different foods too. My greatest joy will be for you to also share in this collective experience and continue to spread love through food.

You will find many of the recipes can be doubled and used as inspiration for quick and easy lunchbox ideas. Interwoven throughout will be recipes from my Korean Canadian upbringing that I now also cook often for my kids, as well as recipes from my mother-in-law and sister-in-law, who taught me cooking can be an amazing and enjoyable family experience.

In many ways, the diversity in this book is like an embodiment of my multiracial children, who are of Korean and Irish heritage. I hope that they will always feel empowered to embrace their cultural differences and identity. In my family, food means love, food means memories, and food is a big part of our cultural identity. I hope that the recipes and inspiration I'm passing along to you will have your picky eaters saying, "More, please!"

— *Jane Kim Nicholson*

As the daughter of Korean immigrants, Jane Kim Nicholson believes in making an impact with food through celebrating and embracing cultural diversity in cuisine. She is the creator, writer, and photographer of the blog and popular Instagram account @Food.Kids.Love, which provides helpful tips and inspiration for simple kid-friendly meals, snacks, and lunches. Jane hails from Canada but currently lives in Los Angeles with her two children, husband, and rescue dog.

HOW THIS BOOK IS ORGANIZED

This book grew out of my heartfelt desire to share what I have learned over the years about preparing nutritious and appealing meals as easily as possible. I strive to create meals that reflect the diversity of my family and are not only nourishing but also enjoyable for my two children. I invite you to join me on an intimate, at-home culinary journey within the pages of this book. Delve into this collection of easy, kid-friendly recipes that aim to please both young palates and the whole family.

LUNCHBOXES

Like most mothers with young children, the daily preparation of school lunchboxes has become an integral part of my routine, so I open this cookbook with a special section on lunchboxes.

Lunchbox Inspiration: This is the pictorial guide to the array of lunchboxes featured in the book. Each image has a page number indicating where you will find details about the lunchbox, including the recipe for the main course in the lunchbox, plus tips on efficient preparation time and ideas to add some fun elements to the lunchbox.

Lunchbox Tips: Notes on ways I have found to make lunchbox prep-and-pack more efficient and hence less stressful. Making lunches can be easy and fun with the right preparation.

Lunchbox Essentials: Suggestions for items and tools that are fun, efficient, and eco-friendly – that help you create an inviting lunchbox that kids will enjoy.

10-Minute Lunchboxes: Ten lunchboxes that take no more than 10 minutes to prepare.

Easy Snack Boxes Five Ways: Five samples of easy-prep snack boxes for after-school sports or other activities, and longer drives.

THE RECIPES

The recipes in the book are arranged in these mealtime sections:

Breakfast, Snacks, Lunch and Dinner, plus a special section on Celebrations.

Within each section are such standards (with my unique touches) as "Triple Berry Bread" (p. 73) interspersed with Korean-inspired creations such as "Mini Korean Sweet Potato 'Doughnut' Muffins" (p. 70). I enjoy blending flavours, as can be seen in "Rice Cake Patties With Edamame and Dried Cranberries" (p. 92), my creative take on rice cakes. I have also included within this collection some Korean and other Asian dishes that you may be familiar with, such as "Korean Gimbap Rolls" (p. 88) and "Tofu Miso Soup" (p. 167).

While this book does not address specific dietary choices and limitations, you will find that there has been a concerted effort to keep the amounts of refined sugar to a minimum. Many recipes are suitable for vegetarians and others who don't eat meat, and vegan, dairy-free, and gluten-free options of some recipes are provided. With many recipes, I include variations to add diversity and kid-friendly tips to make the recipes even more appealing to little ones.

And I wrap up the book with three handy guides:

ASIAN PANTRY

This easy-to-use resource showcases the key ingredients featured throughout the book, allowing you to easily infuse your creations with the distinctive flavours and twists of Asian cuisine.

GLOSSARY OF KOREAN AND OTHER ASIAN TERMS

For ease of reference, I have included a glossary for the terms used in the book.

LUNCHBOX SAFETY

Two registered pediatric dietitian nutritionists explain how to keep lunches on the go healthy and safe and describe common choking hazards for children under the age of 5.

As you join me on this journey to making luscious lunchboxes for your little ones and memorable meals for your entire family, I hope that you will be inspired to create these healthful, fun, and unique recipes that celebrate global flavour. Ultimately, my desire is this book epitomizes its very title: Food *that* Kids Love.

LUNCHBOX INSPIRATION

LUNCHBOX TIPS

Below are some of my most helpful lunchbox tips, incorporating many of my "Lunchbox Essentials" (p. 20), to help you navigate the daily task of packing lunches and ensure a successful school-lunch packing year!

- ✓ Find and purchase a good quality lunchbox that has divided sections, is easy to open and clean, and will last a long time. Stainless steel is a good option. Also useful is a lunchbox with a built-in thermos to pack hot and cold food in one. (See "Lunchbox," p. 20.)

- ✓ Having lunches frozen and ready to go is so helpful, especially on busy mornings. You can prepare and freeze homemade crustless sandwiches (two great options are sunflower/nut butter and jam, and turkey and cheese), veggie waffles, and pizza muffins to name a few.

- ✓ Spend a night washing and cutting fruit and vegetables and storing them in the fridge in jars or containers for easy lunch packing. Place carrots and celery in a container with water to keep them fresh. Prep a variety of fruit in individual jars for easy on-the-go snacking.

- ✓ Try to pack lunches the night before, and make use of leftovers. The best time is right after dinner, while the food is already out. One mess and one cleanup too.

- ✓ Easy school lunch options: the night before, prep a big batch of soup, or make rice in a rice cooker. Or use easy rotisserie chicken to make a big bowl of pasta salad (see Rotisserie Chicken Pasta Salad, p. 106). The salad can last in the fridge for a few days.

- ✓ Shop and take advantage of seasonal fruits and vegetables to build more variety and for optimal taste and nutrition.

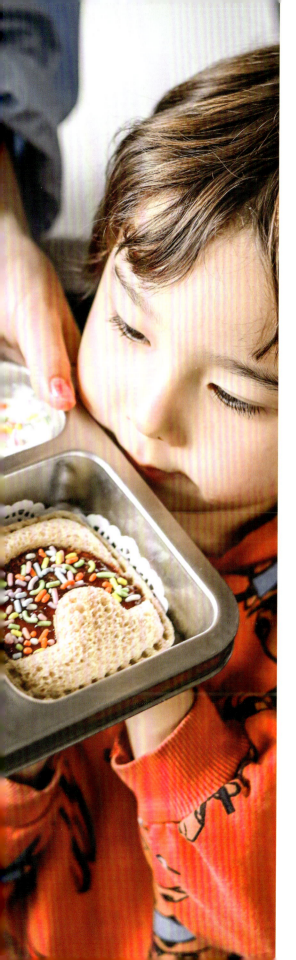

- Use fruit and vegetable cutters to change up the same old vegetable to something more fun! Playful shapes can make such a big difference and help kids try more foods.

- Use kid-friendly food picks to help keep lunchtime at school clean and fun. They are also great tools for picky eaters.

- Have everyone in your household involved in making lunches. If your kids are older, encourage them to start participating in making lunch. Create the system that works best for you and your family.

- But mostly, don't make things over-complicated. Simple is always best. Try not to compare with anyone else, and know we are all doing our very best.

NOTE Ease first-day back-to-school jitters by writing a personal lunchbox note or drawing a silly picture for your little ones to see on their first day of school. Place it in their lunchbox so that when they open it, it's the first thing that they see.

LUNCHBOX ESSENTIALS

Here are some helpful items and tools to make lunchbox prepping easier and more eco-friendly — and the lunches fun to eat. Although not an absolute necessity, keep in mind that most of the products mentioned here are reusable and are made to last a long time. In the long (and short) run, this will save you time and money and also help protect the planet we live on.

CRINKLE CUTTER

This handy little tool cuts fruits and vegetables into a crinkle-cut form. Not only is it useful to help little ones to get a better grip on foods such as avocado, it's also another nice way to subtly transform fruits and vegetables. The wavy shape looks different and is fun for kids. A crinkle cutter can be used for fruits such as apples and avocados, and vegetables such as carrots and potatoes. The crinkle cutter is also a great introductory tool for kids to take part in cooking with you. Once they are able to grip it, they will be able to work right alongside you.

FRUIT AND VEGETABLE FOOD CUTTERS

I call these my "tiny but mighty" tools. If you have a picky eater or if you want to break from your everyday lunchbox, it's nice to stir things up and cut fruits and vegetables into different shapes and forms. You will be surprised at how much this can make a difference. It's also the easiest way to up your creativity in your lunch-packing game! Sometimes, you need to make only one heart-shaped fruit or vegetable to change the whole look of your lunchbox.

LUNCHBOX

My go-to bento-style lunch containers are made of stainless steel because of its sheer durability. I also love that it is non-toxic and less wasteful. Ones with divided sections that can also hold stainless steel dipping containers are ideal. And if it is leakproof, that is also a plus!

It's also practical to have one that comes with a heated thermos section for hot/warm lunches. You may find smaller and more compact lunchboxes more suitable for preschoolers. Just make sure to test out which one is easy for them to open and close on their own.

LUNCHBOX NOTECARDS

Whether it's a handwritten note or a note you can buy in a box, lunchbox notes are a cute way to add a little fun, humour, or inspiration to your child's day. It takes only a minute or two to write but can make a big impression.

RICE BALL MOULD

This may be one of the favourite tools we own. Although you can use your hands to form rice balls, the balls won't come out as perfectly round as they do when you use a rice ball mould. All you have to do is fill the mould with rice and shake back and forth. Your kids will have so much fun with it! Rice balls are a hit with kids and great for snacks, meals, and lunchboxes.

REUSABLE SNACK BAGS

There are many benefits to switching to reusable snack bags. The bags come in food-grade silicone or cloth and in many vibrant colours and kid-friendly designs. Not only are they a better choice for the environment because they replace single-use plastic, they are also durable and built to last a long time. The silicone bags can go in the dishwasher and freezer, and the cloth ones are super easy to wash and dry.

SANDWICH SEALER

We love using our sandwich sealer. It's a convenient lunch-prepping tool to use to make sandwiches in advance and freeze. It also helps keep sandwiches intact so that they are less messy and easier to hold for little ones. Sandwich sealers tend to work better with soft bread. If you don't have a sealer, you can always reinforce the edges of the bread with a fork.

SILICONE LINERS

Silicone liners are a great alternative to paper liners when making muffins, but did you know they also make a great addition to lunchboxes? Mainly they keep food contained and separate and inhibit juices from spilling or leaking into other compartments or adjacent foods. No more soggy sandwiches or wet food to deter your child from eating their lunch. I like to use colourful liners in an otherwise plain lunchbox as another fun way to dress it up. You can even switch up the colours to fit holiday themes, for instance, red for Valentine's Day and orange and black for Halloween.

10-MINUTE LUNCHBOX IDEAS

This is a reminder that lunchboxes can be made in 5 to 10 minutes with the right planning, meal prepping, and ideas. This will ultimately make your busy mornings that much easier. We all need that extra time in the morning!

1. PREP-AND-FREEZE SEALED SANDWICHES

I know that classic PB & J sandwiches don't take much time to make; however, prepping a bunch in advance does have its advantages.

- Even if it's just 5 minutes, it still saves you time and comes in handy for those days where every minute counts.

- Crustless and sealed sandwiches are visually appealing, so chances are better kids will eat them.

- Prepped and ready-made gives direct access and opportunity for kids to pack their own lunchboxes.

- For kids, cut and sealed sandwiches are more fun than a regular sandwich, less messy, easy to pick up and also delicious!

NOTE The key to making these sandwiches is to use a soft whole wheat bread. Take a weekend day, and batch prep with your kids to make the whole week run more smoothly.

Spread any nut butter or sunflower seed butter (if nut-free) and jam in the centre of the bread. Sprinkle seed boosters such as hemp seeds, ground flaxseed, or chia seeds if you wish. Then top with another slice of bread. Place a sandwich sealer on top, and press down firmly. Peel off the crusts, and save them to make croutons or breadcrumbs later. Take a fork and press down on the edges for a tighter seal if need be. Lay sandwiches on a sheet pan, and flash-freeze for 1 to 2 hours; then transfer to a freezer-friendly bag. In the morning, all you need to do is take one out of the freezer, and pack it right into the lunchbox. It will thaw perfectly by lunch. Alternatively, if you want one to eat right away, you can pop it into the toaster!

SEASONAL TIP

Cut sandwiches into rounds, seal, and put two googly eyes on them for a cute Halloween lunch.

2. PREP-AND-FREEZE PIZZA LUNCH

English muffins, pita bread, bagels, and mini naan all work in this recipe. Spread marinara or pizza sauce on top of an English muffin or alternative, layer on shredded mozzarella cheese, and top with desired toppings. To make mini pieces of pepperoni, use a small piping tip and cut out small circles from a bigger pepperoni piece. Once prepped, line pizzas up on a sheet pan, and flash-freeze for 2 hours, and then transfer to a freezer-friendly bag. To reheat, simply place in the oven at 350°F for about 10 to 12 minutes. Alternatively, set your air fryer on the pizza setting (330°F), and air fry for 7 to 8 minutes. While pizzas are heating, assemble the rest of the lunchbox.

SEASONAL TIP

For extra fun, cut pepperoni into heart shapes for Valentine's Day, or make them into cute jack-o'-lanterns for Halloween.

3. FAST AND EASY LUNCH PACKS

Homemade lunch snack packs are my go-to when I need to pack a very quick, 5-minute lunch. It helps to think in compartments, and use a bento-style lunchbox. Although store-bought lunch snack packs are quick and handy, homemade ones have the benefit of you being able to choose what goes in them.

LUNCH SNACK PACK OPTION 1

Layer turkey breast slices with sliced cheddar cheese and whole wheat crackers. Take a star cookie cutter, and cut out cucumbers into stars. Hull and slice strawberries. You can also pack the turkey, cheese, and crackers in separate compartments if your kids want to assemble the lunch on their own and keep the crackers more crispy.

LUNCH SNACK PACK OPTION 2

Pack pretzel thins with prepped Very Lemony Hummus Dip (p. 84), mini bell peppers, and fruit salad with avocado and hemp seeds.

4. MINI EGG SALAD PITAS

Take one night to lunch prep either egg (p. 83), tuna (p. 26), or chicken salad so that these mini pita pockets just need to be filled in the morning. Fill mini pita pockets with desired salad. Pack with a side of carrot sticks, blueberries, and kiwi cut into flowers. To make a flower shape, take a sharp paring knife, cut a zig-zag pattern all around the middle of the kiwi, and slowly pull apart. (Pack with a spoon so that kids can scoop kiwi out with a spoon.)

5. TORTILLA ROLL-UPS

PEANUT BUTTER, STRAWBERRY, AND BANANA ROLL-UPS

Tortilla banana roll-ups are so easy to make in the morning. Just spread nut butter or sunflower seed butter on the tortilla, and add a whole banana on top. Slice strawberries into thin slices, and lean them against the banana. Roll from one end tightly, and slice. The nut butter should act as a seal.

TURKEY (OR CHICKEN) SPINACH PINWHEELS

Take a spinach tortilla wrap, and layer with roasted turkey or chicken slices, purple cabbage, shredded carrots, and mustard. (Prepping your veggies one night of the week is helpful, or buying already shredded cabbage and carrots works too.) Fold in the sides, roll starting from the bottom, and slice. You can use a little cream cheese to act as a seal on the edge.

6. GRILLED TURKEY CHEESE SANDWICH

Butter one side of two slices of bread. Layer cheddar cheese and oven-roasted turkey breast, buttered side out. Heat sandwich in a pan over medium-low heat until golden on both sides and cheese is melted (about 3 minutes per side). Let sandwich cool, cut in half, in fours, in sticks, or even in bite-sized pieces to stick on a skewer. Pack with a paper towel on the bottom to prevent sandwich from getting soggy. Also pictured in this lunchbox are blackberries with halved grapes, cucumber star cut-outs, and hummus.

7. WAFFLED TUNA MELT STICKS

Prep tuna salad ingredients beforehand, and store in the fridge to assemble a quick tuna melt in the morning. Scoop tuna salad on sourdough bread, and top with a slice of cheese. Place sandwich in an oiled or buttered waffle iron, and close lid. Cook for about 4 minutes until cheese is melted and bread is golden in colour.

Tuna Salad

INGREDIENTS

1 can (5 oz) tuna	3 tbsp Greek yogurt
1 tbsp finely diced celery	2 tsp dried cranberries, chopped
1 tbsp finely diced onion	Juice from ½ lemon (about 1 tbsp)
1 tsp Dijon mustard	Salt and pepper

DIRECTIONS

Mix all ingredients together in a bowl. Store in the refrigerator in a sealed container for up to 3 or 4 days.

8. CREAM CHEESE AND STRAWBERRY SANDWICH

Spread cream cheese on bread. Place thinly sliced strawberries on top. Top with another slice of bread spread with cream cheese. Cut in half or in fours.

The sandwich pictured is on ube – purple yam – milk bread, but mini bagels and whole wheat bread are great options. Cream cheese and cucumber is a great alternative.

9. CHICKEN NUGGETS AND CHEDDAR ZUCCHINI WAFFLES

Bake store-bought or prepped homemade chicken nuggets, and pair with Cheddar Zucchini Waffles (p. 32). Pop the waffles in the toaster, and pack with chicken nuggets, leftover corn on the cob, fruit, and a side of ketchup and maple syrup.

10. SESAME RICE BALLS AND EGG

Leftover or freshly cooked rice is easily made into Sesame Rice Balls (p. 90) and will make a nutritious lunch with a hard-boiled egg, vegetables, and seaweed.

EASY SNACK BOXES FIVE WAYS

Here are five simple, on-the-go snack ideas that are virtually no-cook and easy to put together. Snacks do not have to be complicated; the freezer section and even healthy store-bought dips are great options.

1. Dutch pancake bites, yogurt with chia seeds, pistachios, and strawberries

These frozen store-bought Dutch pancake bites take only 10 minutes to warm up in the oven. They are fun to eat with a side of yogurt and fruit. You can also opt to use mini frozen waffles or pancakes. Nuts such as pistachios are great for added protein and good healthy fats. Keep in mind that whole nuts can be choking hazards for children under 5.

2. Pita chips, hummus, cantaloupe balls, celery sticks, and chocolate-covered pretzels

Hummus is made from chickpeas and loaded with nutrients. It's also a great source of protein to keep kids full longer. You can either make a homemade version like our Very Lemony Hummus Dip (p. 84), or go with ease and get a good store-bought version. Cantaloupe is super fun when made into cantaloupe balls with a melon baller. Cut melon into smaller pieces for younger children.

3. Cauliflower pretzel sticks, Colby Jack cheese blocks, crinkle-cut carrot "chips," matchstick apples, and peanut butter dip sprinkled with chia seeds and dye-free sprinkles

Apples cut into matchsticks are fun to dip, and carrots sliced thin into crinkle-cut form changes up the way you serve carrots. Add chia seeds to the peanut butter to add a nutritional boost and dye-free sprinkles to make it a bit more fun and special for kids.

4. Dip, Crunch, and Munch

Get creative with snack dippers to prep beforehand and keep in the refrigerator for easy access.

Peanut butter and apples with a sprinkle of hemp seeds, crinkle-cut carrots and ranch dressing, pretzels dipped in chocolate hazelnut spread with dye-free sprinkles, strawberries paired with peach yogurt dip and chia seeds and a classic crackers with cheese.

5. Mini Sesame Rice Stick Rolls, edamame, sliced dragon fruit, and hard-boiled egg

These mini Sesame Rice Stick Rolls are a version of plain Korean *gimbap* (seaweed rice rolls) that are popular with kids. Dragon fruit is a tasty fruit that is worth trying if you want to break from the norm and introduce something different. Edamame beans are a great source of plant-based protein and are packed with vitamins. They can usually be found in the refrigerated section of stores.

Sesame Rice Stick Rolls

INGREDIENTS

½ cup cooked short-grain white or brown rice

¼ tsp sesame oil

½ tsp sesame seeds

Pinch of salt

1 sheet of roasted seaweed

Sesame oil and sesame seeds for rolls

DIRECTIONS

1. Combine cooked rice with sesame oil, sesame seeds, and salt in a bowl.

2. Cut the seaweed sheet into quarters. Spread a tablespoon of rice on top of half the seaweed sheet. Roll tightly from the bottom end.

3. Brush the outside of the roll with sesame oil, and roll in sesame seeds.

BREAKFASTS

Mornings can be hectic, trying to get everyone, including you, out the door on time, but being prepared with quick, nutritious breakfast ideas can help. From savoury breakfast bowls and Korean egg dishes to twists on classics and make-ahead breakfasts, these recipes can help you make the morning rush a little more manageable — and nourishing.

Rolled Korean-Style Omelette (p. 42)

CHEDDAR ZUCCHINI WAFFLES

These savoury waffles are a blend of my husband's recipe and mine. With the addition of rice flour and scallions, it brings a hint of that Asian flavour that I love so much!

🕐 TOTAL PREP/COOK TIME: 30 MINUTES   🍴 MAKES: 5 LARGE WAFFLES OR 20 SMALL TRIANGLES

INGREDIENTS

1 cup grated zucchini

1 cup grated sharp cheddar cheese

¼ cup diced scallion

1 cup all-purpose flour

¾ cup rice flour

4 tsp baking powder

½ tsp salt

1 tsp garlic powder

2 eggs

⅓ cup avocado oil

2 cups unsweetened almond milk or milk of choice

DIRECTIONS

1. Place the grated zucchini on a paper towel or cheesecloth, and squeeze to remove excess moisture. Set aside with the grated cheddar cheese and diced scallion.

2. In a medium bowl, mix flours, baking powder, salt, and garlic powder. Set aside.

3. Separate the egg yolks and egg whites. With a handheld mixer, beat the egg whites until soft peaks form. (This will make sure your waffles are fluffy!)

4. Add oil and milk to the egg yolks, and whisk.

5. Combine the egg yolk mixture and the dry mixture. Fold in the grated zucchini, grated cheese, and scallion, and mix with a spatula. Fold in the egg whites. Do not overmix.

6. Take 1 cup of batter, and place on preheated, oiled or buttered waffle iron. There will be about ¼ cup of batter per triangle, depending on your waffle iron. Cook for approximately 5 minutes. Repeat until the batter is done.

LUNCHBOX TIP

If you make these ahead of time and freeze them, these savoury waffles make a great lunchbox addition. Place a paper towel in between each layer so that they don't stick together. Just reheat in the toaster in the morning, and pack with some fruit and veggies. You can add a hard-boiled egg for extra protein.

NOTE Serve on a breakfast platter for a fun weekend communal family breakfast. Some breakfast platter add-on ideas include turkey bacon, hard-boiled or fried eggs, fruit, avocado, and, of course, some 100% pure maple syrup! If preparing for a get-together, add edible flowers for a pretty touch.

FLOURLESS APPLE BANANA PANCAKES

These pancakes taste like yummy banana bread without any added refined sugar. The texture is slightly different from a standard pancake – the pancake almost melts in your mouth. My son has been eating these since he was a toddler and still requests them. This pancake recipe can be used in Mini Pancake Yogurt Parfaits (p. 56).

⏱ TOTAL PREP/COOK TIME: 15 MINUTES 🥄 MAKES: 2 TO 4 SERVINGS

INGREDIENTS

2 eggs

1 ripe banana, mashed

¼ cup unsweetened applesauce

½ tsp vanilla

¼ tsp baking powder

½ tbsp flaxseed meal

¼ cup quick oats

Butter or ghee for the pan

DIRECTIONS

1. Add eggs to mashed banana in a small bowl, and mix together.

2. Add the rest of the ingredients with the quick oats last. Mix until combined. Let the batter sit for a few minutes to thicken.

3. Use a tablespoon to scoop batter onto a preheated, oiled or buttered pan on medium-low heat. Cook for about 2 to 3 minutes per side until cooked through and golden in colour.

NOTE The key to keeping these pancakes intact is to keep them mini! Use a solid spatula to flip the pancakes easily. As you progress, the pancakes will keep looking better and better.

ALMOND FRENCH TOAST STICKS

French toast is a good way to use up bread that's past its best-before date. This version uses an air fryer, which makes the toast sticks crispier and saves time. No air fryer? No worries: stovetop method below.

🕐 TOTAL PREP/COOK TIME: 20 MINUTES 🥄 MAKES: 12 STICKS

INGREDIENTS

2 to 3 large slices of day-old bread (sourdough, baguette or any dense bread), cut in 1-inch thick sticks

2 tbsp finely grated almonds

½ tsp cinnamon

¼ tsp freshly grated nutmeg

2 eggs

½ cup extra-creamy unsweetened oat milk or whole milk

1 tsp almond extract

OPTIONAL TOPPING

Sliced cherries, sliced roasted almonds, maple syrup

DIRECTIONS

1. In a medium mixing bowl, combine the ingredients (except bread/toppings), and whisk together well. Dip each stick into the wet mixture, and coat well.

2. Let sticks soak for a few minutes. Place on a lightly oiled air fryer tray.

3. Air fry at 400°F for 8 minutes, turning halfway through.

4. Serve with cherries, almonds, and maple syrup, if using.

STOVETOP METHOD

After coating bread in the wet mixture, place in an oiled or buttered preheated pan over medium-low heat. Cook for about 3 or 4 minutes on each side until fully cooked through and golden in colour.

LUNCHBOX TIP

For younger kids, cut the crust off if it's too crispy. For a fun lunch, cut cooked toast sticks into bite-sized pieces, and layer on skewers with fruit of choice.

SWEET POTATO AND KALE EGG SCRAMBLE

(+ VEGAN OPTION)

Breakfast scrambles are the perfect leisurely weekend breakfast. They're also a great way to use up any leftover vegetables. Sweet potato and kale make a great flavour combo. Change up your egg scramble a bit, depending on your mood, with the option below.

⏱ TOTAL PREP/COOK TIME: 10 MINUTES   🍲 MAKES: 3 TO 4 SERVINGS

INGREDIENTS

Avocado oil for the pan

½ small sweet potato, diced (about ⅓ cup, diced)

¾ cup loosely packed kale, chopped small

6 eggs

3 tbsp water or milk

½ tsp garlic powder

½ tbsp butter

Salt and pepper

DIRECTIONS

1. Wash, peel, and dice sweet potato into small cubes. Wash and chop kale, and set aside.

2. Sauté sweet potato until soft in an oiled pan over medium heat, and then add chopped kale. Sauté for another minute.

3. Whisk eggs in a bowl, and add water or milk. Add garlic powder and salt and pepper to taste.

4. Lower heat to medium-low, add butter, and pour eggs into the same pan.

5. With a spatula, slowly stir the eggs until fully cooked and fluffy (about 2 minutes).

6. Serve right away with toast and fruit of choice.

VEGAN VARIATION

To make this dish plant-based, simply replace the egg with tofu, and make a tofu scramble. Cut tofu into cubes first, and then mix with a wooden spatula until it crumbles. Add spices such as curry and turmeric for extra flavour and colour.

KOREAN STEAMED EGG

(GYERAN JJIM)

Korean steamed egg is a classic childhood dish I grew up eating. It was a communal meal, prepared in a hot stone bowl placed in the centre of the table, and we would happily dip our spoons into it together in one big swoop.

⏱ TOTAL PREP/COOK TIME: 25 MINUTES   🍲 MAKES: 4 SMALL (6 OZ) RAMEKINS

BREAKFASTS: EGG OPTIONS

INGREDIENTS

Sesame oil for the ramekins

4 eggs, whisked

1 tbsp finely diced carrot

½ tbsp finely diced green onion

1 tbsp finely diced broccoli

½ tsp salt

½ cup of chicken or *dashima* (dried kelp) broth (p. 49)

DIRECTIONS

1. Grease 4 small 6 oz ramekins with a little sesame oil. Set aside.

2. Strain the whisked eggs through a fine mesh sieve into a bowl. (This will help achieve a smooth, fluffy, custardy steamed egg.) Add the diced vegetables, salt, and broth to the same bowl, and stir.

3. Fill each prepped ramekin ¾ full with the egg mixture.

4. Fill a separate pot or deep pan ¼ full with water so that when the ramekins are placed in, they are about half submerged in the water. Bring water to a boil, and place the ramekins in the pot.

5. Cover. Lower the heat to medium-low, and let the ramekins steam for approximately 12 minutes.

CAUTION

When removing the ramekins from the pan, use oven mitts or tongs. Ramekins will be hot!

MICROWAVE METHOD

If you are short on time, you can easily make this in a microwave with a similar result. Once you fill the ramekin, place the bowl in the microwave for approximately 2 minutes, and eat right away.

NOTE Eat with a spoon with a Korean side dish such as kimchi. To make kimchi less spicy, simply rinse it. Cut into bite-sized pieces.

BREAKFASTS **41**

KID FRIENDLY TIP

Prepare steamed eggs in individual ramekins so that everyone can have their own. If your kids want to eat the eggs plain without added veggies, that's okay too. You can serve the dish with rice and add separate vegetables and/or *banchan* (Korean side dishes).

ROLLED KOREAN-STYLE OMELETTE

(GYERAN MARI)

Here is another fun way to make eggs using the same ingredients as Korean Steamed Egg (*gyeran jjim*). But instead of steaming, eggs are cooked as if for an omelette, and then rolled and sliced. The egg slices are great for breakfast and are also the perfect lunchbox addition. This recipe has added veggies, but you can make these plain or just add a little diced green onion inside or furikake seasoning on top for flavour.

◷ TOTAL PREP/COOK TIME: 10 MINUTES 🍲 MAKES: 6 TO 8 SINGLE ROLLED OMELETTE SLICES

INGREDIENTS

4 eggs, whisked

1 tbsp finely diced carrot

1 tbsp finely diced broccoli

½ tbsp finely diced green onion (optional)

Salt and pepper

Avocado oil for sautéing

OPTIONAL TOPPING

Furikake seasoning

DIRECTIONS

1. Add the diced vegetables to the eggs. Add salt and pepper to taste. Whisk together.

2. Heat a little avocado oil in the pan over medium-low heat. Make sure not to put the heat on too high. The key is to slowly cook the omelette on medium-low heat so that it still has that beautiful yellow colour.

3. Pour ½ cup of the egg mixture into the pan so that it covers the whole pan. It should resemble the thinness of a crepe. As the egg cooks, start from one end and, using two small spatulas, fold the egg into a roll.

4. When it's rolled halfway, slide the egg to one side. Add another ½ cup of the egg mixture to the empty half of the pan, and begin folding over again to create layers. Repeat until the egg mixture is used up. You should have a tightly rolled layered omelette by the end.

5. Once fully cooked through, let cool slightly, and slice with a sharp knife on an angle diagonally.

LUNCHBOX TIP

A rolled omelette (*gyeran mari*) is a popular Korean lunchbox (*doshirak*) item as it tastes just as good cold as hot. It is also easy to pick up and eat with hands or chopsticks. Pack with Sesame Rice Balls (p. 90) and a side of fresh fruit. This lunchbox has *gyeran mari* with Lemon Turmeric Rice (p. 109), steamed broccoli with sesame oil and furikake seasoning, and watermelon hearts.

KID FRIENDLY TIP

You can customize the vegetables you put in this dish or even omit them altogether, depending on how much time you have and how your children prefer their eggs. Add shredded cheese to change things up a bit.

MUFFIN-TIN EGGS-IN-A-BASKET

These simple and savoury muffin-tin eggs are compact and easy to eat on the go. Halve the recipe to make a smaller batch. If your kids love avocado toast, this spin will have them asking for more!

🕐 TOTAL PREP/COOK TIME: 30 MINUTES   🥄 MAKES: 12 EGGS-IN-A-BASKET

INGREDIENTS

12 slices of dark rye bread, toasted

Olive oil

1 clove garlic, cut in half

2 avocados

Salt and black pepper

Juice from ½ lime

12 eggs

¾ cup grated Parmesan cheese

OPTIONAL TOPPING

Everything Bagel Seasoning mix

Chopped fresh chives

LUNCHBOX TIP

Use a silicone or paper muffin liner to pack these eggs in a lunchbox.

DIRECTIONS

1. Preheat oven to 350°F.

2. Using a cookie cutter or other round shape, cut out a 3-inch circle from each slice of toast. (Use rest of toast for breadcrumbs or croutons.) Brush toast lightly with olive oil, and rub garlic on each piece.

3. Press toast circles in a greased muffin tin. Set aside.

4. In a small bowl, peel and mash avocados. Season with salt and pepper to taste. Add lime and mix.

5. Put a heaping teaspoon of mashed avocado in the middle of each toast cup. Carefully crack an egg into each cup. Sprinkle with Parmesan cheese, and salt and pepper to taste.

6. Bake for 15 to 18 minutes until the egg is cooked through. For extra flavour, sprinkle with seasoning mix or top with chopped fresh chives.

TOFU BREAKFAST BOWL

Classic egg with rice, veggies, and seaweed is always a win! This breakfast bowl is a variation of an egg rice bowl *(gyeran bap)* my mother used to make. Although it's called a breakfast bowl here, it can be made for lunch or dinner.

🕐 TOTAL PREP/COOK TIME: 30 MINUTES 🥣 MAKES: 4 SERVINGS

INGREDIENTS

1 tbsp avocado oil (+ ½ tsp for sautéing spinach)

1 package (14 oz) tofu, drained and squeezed of excess moisture, cut into 1-inch cubes

1 tsp garlic powder

1 tbsp low sodium soy sauce

1 cup spinach

½ tsp sesame oil

3 to 4 cups cooked white or brown short-grain rice

1 sheet of roasted salted seaweed, crushed (*gim* in Korean, *nori* in Japanese)

1 fried egg per bowl

Salt and pepper

Sesame seeds

DIRECTIONS

1. Heat avocado oil in pan over medium heat. Add tofu and garlic powder, and salt and pepper to taste. Cook about 10 to 15 minutes until tofu is golden on all sides.

2. Add the soy sauce and cook for about 2 minutes. Set the cooked tofu aside.

3. Sauté spinach separately until tender, and drizzle with a little sesame oil. Add more salt and pepper if desired.

4. In four individual bowls, layer cooked rice, spinach, crushed seaweed, and tofu. Top with a fried egg. Drizzle a little sesame oil on top, and sprinkle with sesame seeds. Mix with a spoon and enjoy!

LUNCHBOX TIP

If time is short, simply add a fried egg to the rice, and season with a little soy sauce, sesame seeds, sesame oil, and crushed seaweed. Pack in an insulated lunchbox.

KOREAN RICE PORRIDGE WITH BEEF AND VEGETABLES

(SOEGOGI YACHAE JUK)

When my kids are feeling under the weather, the first thing I make them is a bowl of warm Korean rice porridge (*juk*). I try to make this with the same love my mother did when I was little. This porridge is warming to your body, especially when you're not feeling well. And the flavour options of *juk* are pretty endless.

Rice porridge is easily made in either a multi-cooker or in a pot on the stove. This version uses a multi-cooker, so once the ingredients are in, you can go about your morning routine without having to stand over a stove.

🕐 TOTAL PREP/COOK TIME: 20 MINUTES 🥘 MAKES: 4 TO 6 SERVINGS

INGREDIENTS

Avocado oil

⅓ cup finely diced carrot

⅓ cup finely diced zucchini

4 oz thinly sliced sirloin beef in bite-sized pieces

1 tsp sesame oil (+ extra for drizzling)

1 cup uncooked short-grain rice

5 cups *dashima* broth (or chicken/beef broth)

¼ cup frozen corn or peas

Salt

TOPPING

Crushed roasted seaweed

Roasted sesame seeds

Low sodium soy sauce

DIRECTIONS

1. Set your multi-cooker to the SEAR/SAUTE setting, and spray bottom of pot with a little avocado oil. Add the diced carrots and zucchini, and sauté for one minute.

2. Add the beef with sesame oil and salt to taste. Cook for another minute while stirring. Turn off SEAR function.

3. Add 1 cup of uncooked rice with 5 cups of broth in the same pot. Close the lid of your multi-cooker, and pressure cook for 20 minutes on a Custom Setting, or select the Porridge setting.

4. When the cook time is finished, let the pressure naturally release. Once the pressure has naturally released, add the frozen corn or peas, salt to taste, and a drizzle of sesame oil to taste. Stir the porridge.

5. Serve in a small bowl. Sprinkle with roasted sesame seeds and crushed seaweed. Add a tiny drizzle of low sodium soy sauce if desired. Be careful not to add too much. Too much soy sauce will turn your *juk* brown and be overly salty.

Quick and Easy Dashima Broth

INGREDIENTS

5 cups water

3-inch square piece of dried kelp (*dashima*)

DIRECTIONS

Bring water and dried kelp to a boil. Simmer over medium heat for 10 minutes. The dried kelp can also be soaked in water overnight. Use this water to bring out the umami flavour in this dish.

STOVETOP VEGETABLE EGG RICE PORRIDGE

(YACHAE GYERAN JUK)

This is an easy stovetop version of rice porridge.

⏱ TOTAL PREP/COOK TIME: 15 MINUTES   🍲 MAKES: 4 SERVINGS

INGREDIENTS

2 cups cooked short-grain rice

4 to 5 cups chicken broth or
  dashima (dried kelp) broth (p. 49)

¼ cup finely diced carrot

¼ cup finely diced broccoli

¼ cup frozen corn

1 egg, whisked

Salt

TOPPING

Sesame oil

Toasted sesame seeds

Soy sauce (optional)

DIRECTIONS

1. Add cooked rice and vegetables to the broth, and let it come to a boil.

2. Lower heat to medium, and let *juk* cook for a few minutes. Using chopsticks, slowly swirl in the whisked egg. Lower heat and simmer, stirring occasionally. If the liquid is being absorbed too quickly, add a little water as the *juk* cooks. Once the liquid is almost absorbed, the *juk* is ready to eat. Add salt to taste.

3. Drizzle a little sesame oil, and sprinkle with sesame seeds. You can add a tiny bit of soy sauce for extra flavour, but be careful not to add too much, or it will turn murky.

" A day filled with happiness "

KID
FRIENDLY
T I P

Sprinkle some grated cheddar cheese on top while hot if your child loves cheese. It makes the porridge cheesy, gooey, and inviting.

" A day filled with happiness "

THREE COLOURFUL KID-FRIENDLY SMOOTHIES

Smoothies are an excellent way to get some added nutritional boosts into your breakfasts. Here are three tried and true favourite smoothie flavours that my kids ask for on repeat. We just label them as the colour they are: green, purple, or pink!

Green Smoothie
(Mango, Avocado, Spinach)

INGREDIENTS

1 cup frozen mango

1 ripe frozen banana

¼ cup frozen avocado

½ cup spinach

1 cup milk of choice

1 tbsp hemp hearts

TOP WITH CHIA SEEDS OR HEMP HEARTS OR BOTH!

Purple Smoothie
(Blueberry, Peanut Butter, Pineapple)

INGREDIENTS

1 cup frozen blueberries

1 cup frozen pineapple

1 tbsp peanut butter or any nut butter of choice

1 cup milk of choice

¼ tsp cinnamon

TOP WITH AN EXTRA PINCH OF CINNAMON AND CHIA SEEDS!

NOTE For a more efficient smoothie-making process, portion out all the ingredients into individual, freezer-safe bags ahead of time. That way, all you need to do is add your milk of choice in the morning and blend everything together.

Pink Smoothie
(Pitaya, Pineapple, Mango, Mint)

INGREDIENTS

1 dragon fruit (pitaya) smoothie pack (3.5 oz) or frozen pink dragon fruit

1 cup frozen pineapple

½ cup frozen mango

¼ cup Greek yogurt

1 cup milk of choice

1 tbsp hemp seeds

2 fresh mint leaves

TOP WITH CRUSHED PISTACHIOS, AND ADD A MINT LEAF FOR GARNISH.

DIRECTIONS

Combine all the smoothie ingredients in a high-powered blender, and blend for at least 1 minute, or set to a smoothie setting on your blender until fully blended. Pour into a glass, and add extra toppings of your choice. Enjoy right away, or have on the go.

NOTE To make into a smoothie bowl, reduce the milk to ⅓ cup, and top with more fresh fruit and desired toppings. Enjoy with a spoon.

" A day filled with happiness "

BLACKBERRY PEAR CHIA PUDDING

There's something about eating out of a cute little jar that makes all the difference — even to picky eaters. I display the breakfast jars in my fridge, and it never fails: my kids will always reach for them. And what can be better than having breakfast all prepped and ready to go for the week?

🕐 PREP TIME: 5 MINUTES • REST TIME: 2 HOURS OR OVERNIGHT 🍲 MAKES: ONE 6 OZ JAR

INGREDIENTS

1 tbsp chia seeds

¼ cup milk of choice

Dollop of plain or vanilla Greek yogurt

1 to 2 tsp maple syrup, depending on sweetness desired

Diced ripe pear and blackberries

DIRECTIONS

1. In a small jar, combine chia seeds, milk, yogurt, and maple syrup. Stir well.

2. Cover and refrigerate for at least 2 hours or overnight until mixture builds to a pudding-like consistency.

3. When ready to eat, top with diced pear and blackberries. Add more yogurt on top if desired. Give it a good stir and eat!

KID FRIENDLY TIP

Chia pudding is a great way to introduce your kids to different fruits. Try introducing Asian apple pear with its fresh and crunchy consistency. Or have your kids choose their own new fruit to try on your next trip to a farmer's market or your local grocery store.

STRAWBERRIES AND CREAM OVERNIGHT OATS

This is another breakfast jar recipe to prepare ahead. The options and flavour combinations are endless. Any milk will work well, but extra-creamy options are great!

PREP TIME: 5 MINUTES • REST TIME: 2 HOURS OR OVERNIGHT   MAKES: THREE 6 OZ JARS

INGREDIENTS

1 cup traditional rolled oats

1 cup extra-creamy unsweetened oat milk or milk of choice

½ tbsp finely grated almonds

½ tbsp chia seeds

1 to 2 tsp maple syrup, depending on sweetness desired

½ cup diced strawberries

OPTIONAL TOPPING

Nuts, granola, hemp hearts

DIRECTIONS

1. Combine rolled oats, milk, grated almonds, chia seeds, and maple syrup in a bowl. Stir well.

2. Scoop oat mixture into individual 6 oz glass jars, and top with diced strawberries. Secure with a lid, and refrigerate for up to 2 hours or overnight.

3. When ready to eat, add any extra toppings you like, such as nuts or granola, hemp hearts, and more milk, and stir. Enjoy straight out of the jar!

NOTE These recipes are perfect for meal prep. They'll last in the fridge in an airtight jar for up to 4 days, making them a great quick and easy breakfast or snack.

MINI PANCAKE YOGURT PARFAIT

One day, my 10-year-old daughter decided to take mini pancakes and put them in a fancy jar to make a parfait out of them. She layered the mini pancakes with Greek yogurt and topped them with fresh raspberries and then repeated the layers. It looked like a breakfast trifle, drizzled with sweet maple syrup. These parfaits are delicious with a little raspberry compote (p. 62) swirled in too.

⏱ ASSEMBLE TIME: 2 MINUTES   🍳 MAKES: ONE 8 OZ JAR

INGREDIENTS

6 to 8 mini pancakes

½ cup plain Greek yogurt

Fresh raspberries or any fruit of choice

Drizzle of maple syrup

DIRECTIONS

1. In a glass jar, layer 3 or 4 mini pancakes with the Greek yogurt and fruit. Repeat the pancake layers. Drizzle with maple syrup.

2. Enjoy with a spoon!

NOTE We like to use Flourless Apple Banana Pancakes (p. 34) in this parfait, but for a shortcut, you could use your favourite pancake mix to make the pancakes.

TIP For variety, consider adding a layer of zesty lemon curd or experimenting with various fruits to blend new flavours.

SNACKS

Snacks, snacks, and more snacks! Is it just me, or does it feel like kids ask for snacks all day long? How do we try to minimize all-day snacking? Sticking to a routine and having healthy snacks readily available is always a good idea. Prep fresh vegetables and fruit in advance, and have them in the refrigerator for easy access. It will become a total game changer.

In this section, you will find ideas for simple snacks and baked goods that can be prepared ahead of time, including lunchbox snacks, after-school snack ideas, play-date platters with homemade dips, on-the-go snack-box ideas, and healthy snack alternatives.

Very Lemony Hummus Dip (p. 84)

BLACKBERRY VANILLA POPS

I like to have these on hand for a quick and easy snack. Also, kids love the idea of having an ice pop any time of the day! My son likes helping me make these and will gleefully smash the blackberries. The best thing about these is that you can change up the fruit to any flavour you want.

⏱ PREP TIME: 5 MINUTES • FREEZE TIME: 2 HOURS OR OVERNIGHT 🍲 MAKES: 8 (1 OZ) RING POPS

INGREDIENTS

½ cup blackberries

¾ cup vanilla yogurt

1 tbsp all-natural peanut butter or nut butter of choice

OPTIONAL MIX-IN

Granola or crushed graham crackers

Honey

DIRECTIONS

1. Crush the blackberries with a fork or the back of a wooden spoon. Swirl in the yogurt and peanut butter.

2. Add a little honey if you want sweeter ice pops. Put granola or crushed graham crackers on top of the yogurt mixture if desired before placing the stick in.

3. Place into ring pop moulds or any small popsicle mould, and let freeze for at least 2 hours or overnight.

4. Once frozen, simply pop them out of the ice-pop mould and enjoy.

OATMEAL PARFAIT CUPS WITH STRAWBERRY COMPOTE

Top these healthy parfaits with any fruit you like. The optional strawberry compote on top takes it up a notch! For easy mornings, make the oatmeal cups the night before — the next day all you need to do is scoop on the yogurt and top with fruit.

🕐 TOTAL PREP/COOK TIME: 25 MINUTES   🥄 MAKES: 6 MUFFIN-SIZED CUPS

INGREDIENTS

1 large ripe banana, mashed

¾ cup traditional rolled oats

½ tsp vanilla

¼ tsp freshly grated nutmeg

1 tbsp flaxseed meal

TOPPING

½ cup plain Greek yogurt

½ cup diced strawberries or other fruit

Chia seeds

Honey (optional)

Easy Strawberry Compote (optional)

DIRECTIONS

1. Preheat oven to 350°F.

2. In a medium mixing bowl, combine mashed banana with oats, vanilla, nutmeg, and flaxseed meal.

3. Put a heaping tablespoon of batter in a greased silicone muffin mould. Press down so that batter forms a cup, with the edges coming up ¾ high.

4. Bake 15 minutes until golden in colour.

5. Once cooled, carefully pop out the oatmeal cups. Scoop Greek yogurt into the cups, and top with diced strawberries or fruit of your choice. Sprinkle with chia seeds, and finish with a scoop of strawberry compote on top if desired.

VARIATION

To skip the compote step, drizzle honey over yogurt and seeds.

Easy Strawberry Compote

INGREDIENTS

½ cup fresh or frozen strawberries

1 tbsp freshly squeezed lemon juice

1 tbsp maple syrup

2 tbsp water

½ tsp chia seeds

DIRECTIONS

1. Bring ingredients to a boil in a small saucepan. Simmer for 10 minutes until the sauce thickens. Mash the strawberries with a fork to desired consistency.

2. Store in an airtight jar in the refrigerator.

NOTE For Easy Raspberry Compote, substitute raspberries for the strawberries.

SESAME TAHINI GRANOLA BALLS

(GLUTEN-FREE)

The taste of these granola balls is reminiscent of the sesame snaps I enjoyed as a child but without all the refined sugar. The brown rice crisps give a nice crunch, and the tahini and sesame bring out a delicious nutty flavour. These make a great school snack or lunchbox addition and are full of healthy seeds.

⊙ PREP TIME: 10 MINUTES • COOLING TIME: 15 MINUTES MINIMUM 🍴 MAKES: 15 TO 17 GRANOLA BALLS

INGREDIENTS

1 cup gluten-free rolled oats

1 cup gluten-free brown rice crisps

¼ cup tahini

¼ cup honey

1 tbsp hemp hearts

1 tbsp chia seeds

¼ tsp sesame oil

⅛ tsp salt

1 tbsp sesame seeds

¼ cup sesame seeds for rolling

DIRECTIONS

1. In a medium mixing bowl, mix all the ingredients (except for sesame seeds) together starting with the rolled oats. Mix well until the mixture is fully combined.

2. Oil your hands lightly, and take a tablespoon of the mixture into your hands to form a small ball. Be gentle with them. Roll in sesame seeds after forming balls.

3. Place on a small parchment-lined tray or container, and refrigerate for at least 15 minutes before eating. These can be stored in a sealed container in the refrigerator and are ready to eat right away.

NOTE

I like to use oats mixed with ancient grains (quinoa, amaranth, and flaxseed), but using traditional rolled oats is fine.

KID FRIENDLY TIP

This no-cook recipe is a great way to involve kids in the kitchen. They can help pour in the ingredients and roll the granola balls with their hands all in under 10 minutes.

LEMON BLUEBERRY MUFFINS

Blueberries and lemons complement each other so well. No wonder they are a hit with our whole family. They are quick and easy to make, and my kids even prefer them to muffins from the bakery! They also fit perfectly into school lunchboxes.

This makes a small batch of muffins. Double the recipe to make more.

⏱ TOTAL PREP/COOK TIME: 20 MINUTES 🥄 MAKES: 6 MUFFINS

INGREDIENTS

½ cup almond flour

½ cup all-purpose flour

1 tsp baking powder

Pinch of salt

⅓ cup maple syrup

1 egg

¼ cup unsweetened almond milk or milk of choice

½ tsp lemon extract

Zest of ½ lemon (optional)

2 tbsp butter, melted

½ cup fresh blueberries (+ extra for adding on top)

DIRECTIONS

1. Preheat oven to 400°F.

2. Mix the dry ingredients (flours, baking powder, salt) in a medium mixing bowl, and mix the wet ingredients (maple syrup, egg, milk, lemon extract, lemon zest if using) in another. Gradually add butter to wet ingredients.

3. Add the wet ingredients to the dry ingredients, and slowly fold in the blueberries. Mix until just combined. Scoop batter into greased muffin tin. Top with extra blueberries.

4. Bake for approximately 15 minutes until toothpick comes out clean.

MINI STRAWBERRY OATMEAL MUFFINS

This is one of my most popular recipes and for good reason! The muffins are easy to make, and kids love them. I originally made these for my kids when they were toddlers as they make a great toddler snack. But even as my kids have grown, we still make them for a healthy breakfast or snack. They are simply sweetened with bananas and strawberries — no added refined sugar.

⏱ TOTAL PREP/COOK TIME: 20 MINUTES   🥄 MAKES: 18 MINI MUFFINS

INGREDIENTS

⅓ cup diced strawberries
(+ more for sprinkling on top)

1½ ripe bananas, mashed

1½ cups traditional rolled oats

½ cup whole-milk plain yogurt

½ tsp vanilla extract

1½ tsp baking powder

1 tbsp ground flaxseed

DIRECTIONS

1. Preheat oven to 350°F.

2. Wash and dice strawberries, and place in a bowl with mashed bananas.

3. Add the rest of the ingredients (oats, yogurt, vanilla extract, baking powder, ground flaxseed) to the same bowl, and mix together.

4. With a small cookie scoop, scoop muffin batter into a greased mini silicone muffin mould. Fill right to the top.

5. Top with more diced strawberries or a strawberry heart cut-out to be extra fancy.

6. Bake for approximately 15 minutes until done but still moist. Do not overbake. Let cool and enjoy!

VARIATION

These muffins are completely customizable. You can choose to add different fruit (fresh and frozen) and add-ins such as mini chocolate chips, finely grated walnuts ... the list goes on. If you prefer a sweeter muffin, you can add a little maple syrup.

NOTE Store in a freezer-friendly bag or container, and freeze for up to 2 months. Let thaw out on the countertop, or reheat in a microwave for 30 seconds.

MINI KOREAN SWEET POTATO "DOUGHNUT" MUFFINS

(VEGAN)

These "doughnut" muffins are made with Korean sweet potato (*goguma*), first steamed and then baked right into the muffin. The pleasing scent of Korean sweet potato mixed with nutmeg, vanilla, and maple syrup makes the whole house smell like fresh cookies being baked in the oven. The combination of half almond flour and half all-purpose flour gives these muffins a nice consistency, and the fun doughnut shape and mini chocolate chips definitely make these muffins one of my kids' all-time favourite homemade snacks. They are also a perfect addition to the school lunchbox.

⊙ TOTAL PREP/COOK TIME: 25 MINUTES ⬙ MAKES: 16 TO 18 MINI MUFFINS

INGREDIENTS

1 cup mashed Korean sweet potato (about 2 whole potatoes)

1 cup almond flour

1 cup all-purpose flour

1 tbsp baking powder

Pinch of salt

1 tbsp flaxseed meal

¼ cup vegan butter, melted (+ extra for greasing moulds)

¼ cup maple syrup

½ tsp pure vanilla extract

¼ cup unsweetened almond or oat milk

¼ tsp freshly grated nutmeg

¼ cup mini dark chocolate chips

DIRECTIONS

1. Preheat oven to 350°F.

2. Wash, peel, and cut up Korean sweet potatoes into cubes. Place potatoes in a steamer basket on the stove, and steam for 15 minutes until you can pierce through the potato with a fork.

3. In a medium mixing bowl, combine flours, baking powder, salt, and flaxseed meal. In another bowl, mash the cooked sweet potato until smooth, and add melted butter, maple syrup, vanilla extract, milk, and nutmeg. Fold in mini chocolate chips.

4. Grease a mini silicone doughnut pan with a little vegan butter. Put a few mini chocolate chips on the bottom of each mould before scooping 2 tablespoons of batter into the mould. Press down so that the doughnut shape is seen.

5. Bake for 15 to 17 minutes until a toothpick comes out clean.

TRIPLE BERRY BANANA BREAD

If I could choose the perfect banana bread, this would be it. However, the best part of making this banana bread? The sweet smell of bananas wafting through the air, of course.

🕐 TOTAL PREP/COOK TIME: 1 HOUR 30 MINUTES 🍵 MAKES: ONE LOAF

INGREDIENTS

2 eggs

⅓ cup neutral oil (e.g., coconut oil, avocado oil, or butter)

¼ cup unsweetened almond milk or milk of choice

1 tsp vanilla extract

¼ to ⅓ cup organic cane sugar or maple syrup

3 ripe bananas, mashed

1¾ cups all-purpose flour (or 1 cup all-purpose, ¾ cup whole wheat)

1 tsp baking soda

Pinch of sea salt

¼ cup blueberries (+ more for topping)

¼ cup chopped strawberries (+ more for topping)

¼ cup raspberries (+ more for topping)

½ cup crushed walnuts (+ more for sprinkling on top)

DIRECTIONS

1. Preheat oven to 325°F.

2. In a medium mixing bowl, add the wet ingredients (eggs, oil or butter, milk, vanilla extract, sugar or maple syrup), and whisk together. Stir in the mashed banana.

3. In a second bowl, mix together the dry ingredients (flour, baking soda, salt). Pour the dry ingredients over the wet mixture, and mix with a spatula just until combined. Do not overmix. Carefully fold in the berries and the walnuts.

4. Pour mixture into a greased 8 x 4-inch loaf pan, and top with more berries and walnuts. Bake for approximately 1 hour and 20 minutes until toothpick comes out clean. Check after 1 hour as ovens can vary slightly.

KID FRIENDLY TIP

This recipe has added berries for that extra berry goodness, but you can also make it plain. Walnuts add crunch and delicious flavour, but to make it school-safe and nut-free, just omit the walnuts. Chocolate chips are also good, of course.

CRINKLE-CUT KOREAN SWEET POTATO FRIES

Three things that make these fries irresistible: the crinkle cut, the crispiness from the air fryer, and the savoury furikake seasoning. The optional but highly recommended drizzle of honey on top adds even more appeal. The Korean sweet potato (*goguma*) gives it a slightly sweet and nutty flavour. If your kids are still on the fence about sweet potatoes, give this one a try!

⏱ TOTAL PREP/COOK TIME: 20 MINUTES   🥣 MAKES: 4 SERVINGS

INGREDIENTS

2 medium Korean sweet potatoes

1 tbsp cornstarch

1 tsp garlic powder

1 tbsp olive oil

TOPPING

Furikake seasoning

Honey for drizzling (optional)

NOTE If you can't find Korean sweet potato, substitute regular sweet potato.

DIRECTIONS

1. Preheat air fryer to 400°F.

2. Scrub the sweet potatoes, peel if desired, and slice with a sharp knife to desired thickness (about ¼ inch). Using a crinkle cutter, slice in the other direction into sticks.

3. In a medium mixing bowl, combine the crinkle-cut potatoes with the cornstarch, garlic powder, and olive oil. Mix well.

4. Place ½ the batch of potatoes in the air fryer tray, and air fry for 15 minutes, shaking halfway through. (Make sure not to overcrowd the potatoes.) Repeat with the second batch.

5. Sprinkle furikake seasoning on top for a savoury flavour. Then drizzle honey for a little combination of savoury and sweet if desired.

OVEN METHOD

To make these in the oven, simply follow the instructions from steps 1 to 3. Preheat oven to 400°F. Arrange the potatoes on a greased sheet pan (18 x 13 inches), and bake for 20 minutes. Turn the potatoes over, and bake for another 18 to 20 minutes until golden and tender.

SAVOURY KOREAN VEGETABLE PANCAKES

(JEON)

Whenever my mother visits, she stands in front of our stove all day long, sometimes propping herself up on a stool, flipping a variety of Korean pancakes. The scent will be there all day and linger all through the night with a plate of *jeon* always ready, sitting on our counter waiting to be eaten.

These pancakes (*jeon*) are my own version, made with broccoli, corn, and green onion, based on my kids' favourite veggies. But feel free to improvise with whatever vegetables you have on hand. Zucchini, carrots, mushrooms, kimchi, and shrimp are also great additions.

🕐 TOTAL PREP/COOK TIME: 30 MINUTES   🍴 MAKES: 6 TO 8 SMALL PANCAKES

INGREDIENTS

½ cup all-purpose flour

1 tbsp potato starch

1 tsp garlic powder

½ cup cold water

1 egg, whisked

½ cup thinly chopped broccoli

¼ cup thinly sliced onion

¼ cup frozen corn

1 tbsp avocado oil

Salt and pepper

_____

Tangy Soy Sauce Dip

DIRECTIONS

1. Combine the dry ingredients (flour, potato starch, garlic powder, salt and pepper to taste) with the water and egg in one bowl.

2. Sauté broccoli and onion. Add corn to the flour and egg mixture and stir until combined

3. Heat avocado oil in pan. Place a heaping tablespoon of batter, spread thinly, in the pan. Cook over medium heat for about 2 minutes on each side. (Lower heat slightly if it gets too hot.) Add more oil in between batches.

4. Slice into triangles, and serve hot with a side of Tangy Soy Sauce Dip.

Tangy Soy Sauce Dip

INGREDIENTS

1 tbsp low sodium soy sauce

½ tbsp water

1 tsp rice vinegar

½ tsp sesame oil

½ tsp sesame seeds

½ tsp finely sliced scallions (optional)

DIRECTIONS

Combine all the ingredients in the order listed in a small dipping bowl.

Once cooled, these pancakes can be packed right into a lunchbox.

RICE CAKES WITH MARINATED BEEF

(BULGOGI TTEOKBOKKI)

Chewy, savoury, and slightly sweet, these rice cakes (*tteokbokki*) are the ultimate Korean comfort food. Technically, they can be considered a whole meal as they can be quite filling, depending on how many pieces you have. This is a non-spicy version that I enjoyed when I was a child. If you ever have leftover *bulgogi* (Korean marinated beef), this is the perfect dish to make with it.

⏱ PREP TIME: 10 MINUTES • MARINATING TIME: 30 MINUTES OR OVERNIGHT
• COOK TIME: 10 MINUTES 🍲 MAKES: 6 SERVINGS

INGREDIENTS

1.5 lb cylindrical rice cake

8 oz sirloin beef, thinly sliced

Sesame oil for pan (+ ½ tsp)

1 small onion, sliced

1 bell pepper, sliced

1 carrot, sliced into ¼ inch ovals or julienned

Salt and pepper

1 cup water

TOPPING

Roasted sesame seeds

Sliced green onions

DIRECTIONS

1. If using frozen rice cakes, soak rice cakes in a bowl of water for at least 15 to 20 minutes. Drain and set aside. Prepare *tteokbokki* (rice cake) sauce, and set aside.

2. Marinate thinly sliced beef in the Sirloin Beef Marinade (p. 79) for at least 30 minutes or overnight in the refrigerator.

3. Over medium heat in an oiled pan, stir-fry the sliced vegetables until tender (about 3 to 4 minutes), add salt and pepper to taste, and set aside. Stir-fry the marinated beef for 3 to 4 minutes until cooked through. Remove from pan and set aside.

4. Add 1 cup of water to the stir-fry pan, and bring to a quick boil. Add the rice cakes and the prepared *tteokbokki* sauce. Lower heat, and simmer for about 5 minutes, stirring occasionally. Stir in the sautéed vegetables and beef. (The liquid should have slowly thickened.)

5. Drizzle ½ tsp sesame oil on the mixture at the end, and sprinkle with roasted sesame seeds before serving. Garnish with sliced green onion if desired.

Sirloin Beef Marinade
(BULGOGI MARINADE)

INGREDIENTS

2 tbsp low sodium soy sauce

2 tbsp water

2 tsp sesame oil

2 tsp minced garlic

2 tbsp honey

½ tsp grated ginger

2 tbsp grated apple or Asian apple pear

2 tsp roasted sesame seeds

Black pepper to taste

DIRECTIONS

Mix all ingredients well.

Rice Cake Sauce
(TTEOKBOKKI SAUCE)

INGREDIENTS

1½ tbsp low sodium soy sauce

1 tbsp apple cider vinegar

2 tbsp honey

1 tbsp sesame seeds

1 tsp sesame oil

DIRECTIONS

Mix all ingredients well.

MUFFIN-TIN SNACK TRAY

Kids can be encouraged to eat their fruits and veggies if they have something fun to dip with! And muffin-tin platters are a great way to present fruits and vegetables in a new way, especially for play dates or small get-togethers with friends. These two dips are great for dipping fruit, pretzels, and crackers. Cherry tomatoes, carrots, and celery are delicious dippers too. Cut apples into fun sticks for easy dipping for everyone.

⏱ PREP TIME: 5 MINUTES PER DIP 🍯 MAKES: ONE 6 OZ RAMEKIN PER DIP

Raspberry or Strawberry Cream Cheese Chia Dip

INGREDIENTS

1 tbsp freeze-dried raspberries or strawberries, finely ground

½ cup cream cheese, softened

1 tsp chia seeds

½ tsp maple syrup

DIRECTIONS

Fold the ground berries, chia seeds, and maple syrup into the cream cheese. Mix well together.

Almond Butter Yogurt Dip

INGREDIENTS

1 tbsp finely ground roasted almonds

½ cup plain Greek yogurt

1 tbsp almond butter

½ tsp honey

TOPPING

Grated milk or dark chocolate

DIRECTIONS

1. Add the ground almonds to the yogurt along with the almond butter and honey. Mix well until combined.

2. Grate the desired amount of milk or dark chocolate on top.

NOTE Make sure to cut fruit and tomatoes into smaller pieces to avoid choking hazards for younger kids under 5 years old. Provide softer cracker alternatives as well.

KID-FRIENDLY TEA SANDWICHES

Tiny tea sandwiches are my go-to when making snack platters for kids. Snack platters are visually appealing, and there is a lot of room for variety. Snack platters also provide a good opportunity to include different vegetables with a protein-rich dip. Cute and tasty tea sandwiches just take it up a notch, and they're perfect for little hands and for the lunchbox.

Mini Cucumber Dill Cream Cheese Sandwiches

🕐 PREP TIME: 10 MINUTES
🍵 MAKES: 6 ROUND TEA SANDWICHES

INGREDIENTS

6 slices of soft whole wheat bread

2 oz cream cheese (about 3 tbsp)

½ tsp chopped fresh dill

6 slices of English cucumber, very thinly sliced

Black pepper (optional)

DIRECTIONS

1. Cut 12 circles out of bread using a 2-inch round cookie cutter.

2. Combine cream cheese and dill. Spread dilled cream cheese on each bread circle, and layer half the circles with a slice of cucumber. Add cracked black pepper on top if desired.

3. Top with another slice of cream cheese-spread bread, with the filling facing in.

Egg Salad Tea Sandwiches

🕐 TOTAL PREP/COOK TIME: 20 MINUTES
🍵 MAKES: 9 RECTANGULAR TEA SANDWICHES

INGREDIENTS

4 eggs

1 tbsp mayonnaise

½ tsp Dijon mustard

¼ to ½ tsp chopped fresh dill

Salt and pepper

6 slices of soft bread (Korean- or
   Japanese-style milk bread works well)

DIRECTIONS

1. Hard-boil eggs. Peel eggs, and mash
   with a potato masher. Add mayonnaise,
   Dijon mustard, fresh dill, and salt and pepper
   to taste. Mix well.

2. Cut crusts off bread. Spread egg salad on
   half the slices of bread. Top with remaining
   slices. Cut each sandwich into 3 rectangles.

VERY LEMONY HUMMUS DIP

(VEGAN + GLUTEN-FREE OPTION)

This hummus gets its peppy lemony zing from a whole juiced lemon, lemon olive oil, and a little lemon zest!

⏲ PREP TIME: 5 TO 10 MINUTES   🥄 MAKES: 6 SERVINGS

INGREDIENTS

1 can (15.5 oz) chickpeas

¼ cup water or aquafaba (liquid from chickpeas)

¼ cup tahini

Juice of one lemon (reduce to ½ lemon for a milder lemon flavour)

1 clove garlic

1 tbsp low sodium soy sauce (use coconut aminos for gluten-free)

2 tbsp lemon olive oil

Salt

OPTIONAL TOPPING

½ tsp lemon zest

Paprika

DIRECTIONS

1. Reserve ¼ cup of the liquid (aquafaba) from chickpeas. Set aside. Drain the rest of the liquid, and rinse chickpeas.

2. In a high-powered blender or food processor, add tahini and juice of one lemon. Add chickpeas, garlic, soy sauce, lemon olive oil, and salt to taste. Grind until smooth, at least 2 minutes.

3. As mixture is being processed, slowly add the reserved ¼ cup of aquafaba or cold water until consistency is creamy.

4. Top with a sprinkle of paprika and a little lemon zest, if desired, for an extra lemony flavour.

MEALS FOR THE WHOLE FAMILY

Sometimes, preparing lunches and dinners can be an overwhelming task — especially after a long day at work or on a busy morning. Following are some easy recipes that I make often for my family, tried and true recipes that my kids love — and many transfer well for lunch leftovers the next day. You will find a little bit of everything, including simple recipes with an Asian twist.

Slow Cooker Spicy Chicken
and Potato Stew (p. 124)

KOREAN GIMBAP ROLLS

This is a simple version of *gimbap* that I often make for my kids. The options of what you can put inside are endless. I kept this one simple with egg, cooked carrots, cucumber, and pickled daikon radish. But you can also use other ingredients, for example, fish cake, tuna, and *bulgogi* (p. 78) to amplify taste and flavour! If you have any *gimbap* left over, you can dip the pieces in whisked egg and pan-fry over medium-low heat until both sides are cooked.

🕐 TOTAL PREP/COOK TIME: 30 MINUTES   🥢 MAKES: 4 ROLLS (10 PIECES PER ROLL)

INGREDIENTS

3 cups cooked short-grain rice, cooled

1 tbsp sesame oil (+ more for sautéing and drizzling)

1 tbsp sesame seeds

Salt

½ cup julienned carrots

½ English cucumber

4 strips pickled daikon radish (*danmuji*)

4 sheets of roasted, unsalted seaweed

2 eggs

KID FRIENDLY TIP

If your child is not ready to eat *gimbap* rolls, try serving them deconstructed. You can serve the egg, cucumber, carrot, and daikon on a plate separately with some mini Sesame Rice Stick Rolls (p. 29).

DIRECTIONS

1. Add sesame oil, sesame seeds, and salt to taste to rice. Mix together, and set aside.

2. Sauté carrots in a pan until cooked. Drizzle the carrots with a little sesame oil and sprinkle with a little salt. Set aside.

3. Peel and cut cucumber in half. Remove seeds with a spoon, and slice cucumber into 4 thin strips. Set aside. Slice pickled radish into thin strips (or buy pre-cut at a Korean market). Set aside.

4. Whisk two eggs in a bowl, and pour into a heated, oiled pan over medium-low heat. Let the egg spread thinly to cover the whole pan, and cook for 1 to 2 minutes. Flip it over to cook the other side (about 30 seconds), and then slice in 1-inch strips. Set aside.

5. Place seaweed sheet shiny side down on top of a bamboo sushi mat. Using a rice paddle, spread rice on top of half the sheet starting from the bottom. Layer the toppings in the middle of the rice.

6. From the bottom, grab both the sushi mat and the seaweed with rice and fillings, and start to roll the sushi upward tightly. Once you get to the end, seal the end by brushing some water with your fingertip along the edge of the seaweed sheet, and roll tightly. Using a silicone brush, brush the roll lightly with a little sesame oil. Repeat with remaining sheets of seaweed.

7. Slice, using a SHARP, wet knife.

SESAME RICE BALLS

Rice balls are perfect to pack in a lunchbox because they are easy to hold and eat. They are also super quick and simple to make, and you can customize the flavours by adding virtually anything you want. Here is a good base recipe to start with. The sesame oil and furikake seasoning bring out a subtle but savoury flavour.

🕐 PREP TIME: 10 MINUTES 🥄 MAKES: 14 RICE BALLS

INGREDIENTS

1 cup cooked short-grain rice, cooled slightly

1 tsp sesame oil

½ tbsp furikake seasoning or to taste

Salt

DIRECTIONS

1. Scoop cooked rice into a small mixing bowl. Add sesame oil, furikake seasoning, and salt to taste to the rice, and mix well.

2. Scoop 1 tablespoon of rice per ball into a rice ball mould, and close the lid.

3. Shake the rice ball mould back and forth for about 15 seconds until a nice round ball is formed.

VARIATION

Salmon, beef (*bulgogi*) (p. 78), and finely chopped vegetables are all great add-ins to these rice balls and a good way to use up leftovers. Children love picking these up and eating with their hands.

The Sesame Rice Balls pictured here have salmon mixed in with the rice. You can use fresh cooked salmon or canned salmon. Either works well.

KID FRIENDLY TIP

Let your children help by measuring and adding the ingredients. They can also help with mixing and then shaking the mould back and forth. This recipe is so easy that soon they will be making these on their own.

NOTE If you don't have a rice ball mould, simply use your hands to form a ball. Oil hands slightly with a little sesame oil to prevent sticking.

RICE CAKE PATTIES WITH EDAMAME AND DRIED CRANBERRIES

I created these rice cake patties based on a favourite salad recipe I love. The dried cranberries give a subtle, chewy sweetness and pair well with the edamame beans. These are easy to pack for school lunches and are also very quick to make on busy weeknights.

🕐 TOTAL PREP/COOK TIME: 15 TO 20 MINUTES   🥄 MAKES: 16 SMALL PATTIES

INGREDIENTS

2 cups cooked short-grain rice

1 tsp sesame oil

⅓ cup panko bread crumbs

1 tsp garlic powder

2 tbsp dried cranberries

2 tbsp edamame, shelled

2 eggs

¼ cup grated Parmesan cheese

1 tsp parsley

Salt and pepper

1 tbsp avocado oil

DIRECTIONS

1. Combine the ingredients, except for the avocado oil, in a medium mixing bowl. Add salt and pepper to taste, and mix well.

2. Take a heaping tablespoon of the mixture, and form into small round patties.

3. Heat avocado oil in a pan over medium heat. Place patties in the pan, and cook for 2 to 3 minutes per side until golden brown.

KID FRIENDLY TIP Serve with a side of sour cream or Tangy Soy Sauce Dip (p. 76).

MINI SWEET POTATO MAC 'N' CHEESE BITES

Something about being bite-sized and mini always makes these a hit with the kids. The added sweet potato gives more nutrient value to the mac and cheese. I like to make these as a fun appetizer for kids for Thanksgiving and other special meals. They also make a great lunchbox item. You will need a mini muffin tin to make these. Also, a silicone muffin tin makes these bites easy to pop out.

⏱ TOTAL PREP/COOK TIME: 35 MINUTES   🥣 MAKES: 42 MINI BITES

INGREDIENTS

1 large sweet potato, peeled and roughly chopped

4 cups cooked elbow pasta

¼ cup unsweetened almond milk or milk of choice

1 tsp paprika

Salt

½ cup shredded white cheddar cheese (+ more for sprinkling on top)

⅓ cup panko bread crumbs

DIRECTIONS

1. Preheat oven to 375°F. Cook elbow pasta according to package instructions.

2. Steam sweet potato chunks for about 15 to 18 minutes until they can be pierced easily with a fork. Mash sweet potato with a potato masher, and then add milk, paprika, and salt to taste.

3. Combine cooked pasta with the sweet potato mash, and mix well. Add the cheddar cheese, and mix again.

4. Scoop into a greased mini muffin tin, filling each cup all the way to the top. Sprinkle with panko bread crumbs and the desired amount of additional cheese. Bake for 15 minutes until golden brown.

LUNCHBOX TIP

These bites taste just as good the next day and are easy for kids to pick up and eat for lunch at school. Set some aside the night before, and refrigerate to add to your child's lunchbox in the morning.

MINI SALMON CAKES

We like making these mini salmon cakes for a quick and easy lunch. Having a batch ready in the freezer to pack in lunchboxes in the morning also comes in handy. These salmon cakes are great for little hands and for dipping! My kids love eating these with a side of rice and sliced cucumbers or cucumber salad.

🕐 TOTAL PREP/COOK TIME: 15 MINUTES 　🍳 MAKES: 8 MINI PATTIES

INGREDIENTS

1 can (6 oz) wild pink salmon

2 tbsp whole wheat or panko bread crumbs

1 egg

½ tsp garlic powder

½ tsp paprika

1 tsp finely chopped fresh dill

Salt and pepper to taste

1 tbsp avocado oil for the pan

—————————

Avocado Dill Dip

DIRECTIONS

1. Combine all the ingredients (except for the avocado oil and dip) in a medium bowl, and mix well. Using a tablespoon scoop, gently form small round patties with your hands.

2. Heat avocado oil in a pan. Over medium heat, cook the patties for about 2 minutes on each side until nicely browned. Lower the heat if necessary halfway through if patties are getting too browned.

FREEZER TIP

Can be stored in the freezer for up to 2 months. Let cooked salmon patties cool completely, and then flash-freeze on a sheet pan for at least 1 hour. Transfer to a freezer-friendly bag or container.

TO REHEAT

Let thaw in the refrigerator, and warm briefly in a heated oven or microwave.

Avocado Dill Dip

INGREDIENTS

½ cup Greek yogurt

½ avocado, mashed

Juice from half a lemon

1 tsp finely chopped fresh dill

1 clove garlic, minced

Salt

DIRECTIONS

Combine all the ingredients in a bowl, add salt to taste, and mix together well. Store in an airtight container in the refrigerator for up to 3 days.

AIR FRYER SALMON TERIYAKI BITES

When it comes to weeknight dinners, simple is always best. This recipe takes very little prep time, and with the help of the air fryer, dinner will be ready before you know it.

⏱ TOTAL PREP/COOK TIME: 15 MINUTES • MARINATING TIME: 15 MINUTES (MINIMUM) • 🍴 MAKES: 4 SERVINGS

INGREDIENTS

1 lb wild-caught salmon

Avocado oil spray for air fryer

FOR THE MARINADE

¼ cup low sodium soy sauce

1 tbsp rice wine vinegar

2 tsp sesame oil

1 tsp oyster sauce

2 tbsp sesame seeds (+ extra for garnish)

½ tsp fresh minced ginger

1 clove garlic, minced

1 tbsp maple syrup or honey

DIRECTIONS

1. Cut salmon into bite-sized pieces (1-inch cubes), and place in a medium mixing bowl.

2. Measure the marinade ingredients into a jar, shake well, and pour over the salmon. Cover and let marinate for at least 15 to 30 minutes or overnight.

3. Spray air fryer tray with a little avocado oil. Air fry salmon at 400°F for approximately 10 minutes until fully cooked through.

4. Add extra sesame seeds on top for garnish.

STOVETOP METHOD

Heat 2 teaspoons of avocado oil over medium heat. Add marinated salmon chunks to the pan, and cook for approximately 4 to 5 minutes, gently flipping halfway, until cooked through. Sprinkle more sesame seeds on top.

NOTE Serve with rice and a side of roasted or steamed vegetables. Store leftovers in an airtight container in the refrigerator for up to 3 days.

ELLA

LETTUCE DRESS PLATE

HAVE FUN WITH FOOD!

Sometimes, it takes a little creativity to get your kids to try new foods — especially when it comes to green vegetables and different fruits. Try using different props such as this cute personalized plate with fun cut-outs, and give your kids the ingredients and tools to get creative on their own. My daughter (a fashion designer in the making!) made this fancy lettuce dress out of romaine lettuce, sprinkled on some diced bell peppers for decoration, and used a dragon fruit for the top. She added some blueberries and strawberries as earmuffs and included a cut-out strawberry heart for the middle of the top. So simple but so effective! When my younger one saw it, he begged to eat it. Of course, she shared, even if at first it was reluctantly.

Everyday Honey Mustard Dressing

INGREDIENTS

3 tbsp olive oil

1 tbsp white or red wine vinegar

1 tbsp honey

½ tbsp Dijon mustard

1 clove garlic, minced

Salt and pepper to taste

DIRECTIONS

Mix all the ingredients together in a jar, and shake well. Pour over salad and toss.

KID FRIENDLY TIP

Place a salad dressing or dip on the side so that kids can dip their vegetables into it. That way, they can control how much dressing is on their salad.

Try the Cabbage Salad Dressing (p. 115) and the Avocado Dill Dip (p. 96) on salads, or shop around for store-bought dressings that your kids might like, and use them.

MACARONI SALAD SWEETENED WITH HONEY

(+VEGAN OPTION)

Summer isn't summer without macaroni salad. This recipe is the perfect balance of not too creamy, not too sweet — just the right amount of everything to pair with all your kids' summertime barbecue favourites. Bring it to your next potluck, or make it in advance to pack as a side in your kids' lunchboxes. Make sure to always pack with an ice pack.

🕐 PREP TIME: 20 MINUTES 🥄 MAKES: 8 SERVINGS

INGREDIENTS

4 cups cooked elbow pasta, rinsed

2 tbsp finely diced red and orange bell pepper

2 tbsp finely diced celery

2 tbsp finely diced carrot

1 tbsp finely diced red onion

2 hard-boiled eggs, whites and yolks separated

⅓ cup vegan mayonnaise

1 tsp Dijon mustard

1 tbsp honey or maple syrup

1 tbsp white wine vinegar

Salt and pepper

Parsley for garnish

DIRECTIONS

1. In a medium mixing bowl, whisk together the mayonnaise, Dijon mustard, honey, white wine vinegar, and salt and pepper to taste.

2. Stir the diced vegetables into the prepared dressing. Add the macaroni. Chop the hard-boiled egg whites, and mix together gently.

3. Grate the hard-boiled yolks on top, and sprinkle on some parsley if desired.

4. Cover and let cool in the refrigerator until ready to eat.

VEGAN VARIATION

Omit the hard-boiled eggs, and use maple syrup instead of honey.

KOREAN-INSPIRED POTATO SALAD

The hard-boiled egg whites and sweet apples give this potato salad the distinct flavour that I knew as a child. This is still one of my favourite simple side dishes and a great way to add fruit and vegetables to your child's meal. There is also a mashed version that is quite popular, but I prefer this chunkier version.

⏱ TOTAL PREP/COOK TIME: 30 MINUTES 🍲 MAKES: 6 SERVINGS

INGREDIENTS

2 large potatoes (3 cups), peeled and cut into small chunks

½ cucumber (about ½ cup), cut into small chunks

2 carrots (about ½ cup), cut into ¼ inch coins

1 apple (about 1 cup), cut into small chunks

6 hard-boiled eggs, quartered (set aside one yolk)

½ cup mayonnaise (vegan, regular, or Kewpie)

2 tbsp Greek yogurt

Salt and pepper

DIRECTIONS

1. Boil potatoes and carrots together in salted water until you can pierce them with a fork (about 10 minutes). Do not overcook. Drain and set aside.

2. Combine the potatoes, cucumber, carrots, apples, and hard-boiled eggs in a medium mixing bowl. Add mayonnaise, Greek yogurt, and salt and pepper to taste. Mix gently.

3. Finally (a tip I learned from my mom), grate the hard-boiled egg yolk that was set aside on top of the potato salad. Chill before serving.

VARIATION

To make a mashed version, omit the cucumbers. Mash the potatoes and eggs together, and combine with finely diced apples and carrots. Combine with mayonnaise and Greek yogurt, and season with salt and pepper to taste. Scoop with an ice cream scoop!

ROTISSERIE CHICKEN PASTA SALAD

🕐 TOTAL PREP/COOK TIME: 15 MINUTES   🍲 MAKES: 6 SERVINGS

INGREDIENTS

1 package (8 oz) tri-coloured pasta

¼ cup diced onion

¼ cup sweet pimentos

½ orange bell pepper (about ⅓ cup), diced

¼ cup sliced black olives

1 cup rotisserie chicken, chopped

DRESSING

3 tbsp olive oil

1 tbsp red wine vinegar

1 tsp garlic and Italian seasoning

1 tsp chopped fresh basil

½ tsp honey

Salt and pepper

DIRECTIONS

1. Cook pasta according to package instructions. Drain and rinse.

2. Shake dressing ingredients together well with salt and pepper to taste in a jar with a tight-fitting lid.

3. Combine pasta, vegetables, sliced olives, and chicken in a medium salad bowl. Add the dressing and toss. Season with salt and pepper to taste. Refrigerate and serve cold.

LUNCHBOX TIP

To make lunchbox packing easier, prep a batch of pasta salad at the beginning of the week, so you will have salad ready when you need it.

SHEET PAN CHICKEN AND ROASTED VEGETABLES WITH LEMON TURMERIC RICE

Sheet pan dinners are always helpful on busy weeknights. This dish has savoury Greek flavours that my kids and I love. And the lemon turmeric rice is one of our favourites, made super easy in a rice cooker.

🕐 TOTAL PREP/COOK TIME: 30 MINUTES • MARINATING TIME: 30 MINUTES (MINIMUM) 🍴 MAKES: 4 SERVINGS

INGREDIENTS

2 boneless chicken breasts (1 lb), cut into 2-inch pieces

2 cups chopped vegetables (e.g., zucchini, squash, onion, bell pepper, broccoli)

1 tsp olive oil

½ tsp paprika

½ tsp granulated garlic

Salt and pepper

MARINADE FOR CHICKEN

3 tbsp olive oil

1 tsp basil

1 tsp thyme

1 tsp oregano

½ tsp rosemary

Juice from 1 lemon

1 tsp fresh chopped dill

Salt and pepper

DIRECTIONS

1. Combine the marinade ingredients in a jar with a lid, with salt and pepper to taste, and shake well. Pour marinade over chicken, cover, and let marinate for at least 30 minutes or overnight in the fridge.

2. Preheat oven to 400°F.

3. Toss the vegetables with olive oil, paprika, garlic, and salt and pepper to taste. Place chicken on a sheet pan with the vegetables. (Make sure not to overcrowd.)

4. Bake for 18 to 20 minutes until chicken is fully cooked, turning halfway through. Lastly, put the tray under the broiler for 2 to 3 minutes until nicely browned.

Simple Rice Cooker Lemon Turmeric Rice

INGREDIENTS

2 cups basmati or jasmine rice

2 ½ cups chicken broth

1 tsp turmeric

1 tsp garlic powder

Salt and pepper

Juice from 1 lemon

DIRECTIONS

1. Wash and drain rice a few times with cold water until the water runs clear. Put rice in rice cooker, and add the chicken broth. Add turmeric, garlic powder, salt and pepper to taste, and mix.

2. Select the white rice option on the rice cooker, and set to start. Once the rice is cooked, open the rice cooker, and squeeze in lemon juice. Fluff rice with a rice paddle.

STOVETOP METHOD

For 2 cups of rice, add 3 ½ cups of broth. Add spices, including salt and pepper to taste. Bring to a boil, and cover with lid. Reduce heat to a low simmer, and cook for 15 minutes. Add lemon juice. Fluff rice with a rice paddle.

SWEET POTATO EGG FRIED RICE

(SWEET POTATO OMURICE)

This dish will always remind me of my childhood. I would run home after school and be greeted with the familiar scent of rice and veggies sizzling in a pan. My mother would make a thin, crepe-like egg that would fold neatly over the colourful fried rice. I would then top it with a dollop of ketchup. I couldn't wait to dig in. I love that now my kids are creating their own version of these memories.

⏱ TOTAL PREP/COOK TIME: 25 MINUTES 🍚 MAKES: 6 TO 8 SERVINGS

INGREDIENTS

1 small sweet or white potato, diced (about 1 cup diced)

½ cup diced zucchini

¼ cup diced carrot

⅓ cup diced celery

1 tbsp diced onion

½ cup frozen corn, thawed

1 tbsp avocado oil

4 cups cooked and cooled short-grain rice (day-old rice works well)

1 tbsp low sodium soy sauce

Salt and pepper

2 tsp sesame oil

2 tbsp sesame seeds

1 egg + 1 tsp water per serving

Ketchup or hot sauce for serving

DIRECTIONS

1. Mix vegetables (except for the potato and corn) together, and set aside.

2. Heat avocado oil in a large pan or wok, and sauté the potato for 3 to 5 minutes until soft. Add the rest of the diced vegetables, and sauté for another 3 to 4 minutes until cooked through. Lower heat, and add rice and corn. Sauté for another minute.

3. Add the soy sauce, and mix until well combined. Add salt and pepper to taste.

4. Drizzle with sesame oil, and sprinkle sesame seeds on top, and mix.

FOR THE EGG

For each serving, crack an egg in a small bowl. Add 1 teaspoon of water and salt to taste, and whisk well. Over medium-low heat, pour egg into a heated, oiled pan to make a thin layer. Cook for a couple of minutes, and then flip over for another 30 seconds to cook evenly. Make sure to prevent over-browning.

TO SERVE

Place the cooked egg on a plate. Scoop fried rice on one half of the egg. Carefully fold the egg over the rice, and top with a little ketchup (or hot sauce for grown-ups and older kids). Sprinkle with more sesame seeds. Enjoy!

LUNCHBOX TIP

Pack leftover fried rice, heated, in the thermos section of your child's lunchbox. To add an egg, quickly scramble an egg right into the fried rice. Small, leakproof condiment containers are great to have on hand to pack a side of ketchup.

KIMCHI KALE FRIED RICE WITH TUNA

Kimchi is a staple in our household. It's something we always have in our fridge no matter what. The best part of kimchi is when it starts to ripen — signalling for me it's time to make kimchi fried rice. To make kimchi kid-friendly, simply rinse the kimchi with water to remove the spice. My daughter, now that she's older, has graduated to eating this spicier version. The non-spicy version is perfect for my son.

🕐 TOTAL PREP/COOK TIME: 15 MINUTES 🍚 MAKES: 8 SERVINGS

INGREDIENTS

Avocado oil

1½ cups chopped kimchi

1 cup finely chopped kale

1 can (6 oz) tuna

1 to 2 tsp Korean hot pepper paste (*gochujang*)

½ tsp Korean chili flakes (*gochugaru*) (optional)

4 cups cooked short-grain rice (day-old rice works well here)

1 to 2 tbsp kimchi juice (liquid from the kimchi container)

1 tbsp sesame oil

2 tbsp sesame seeds

Fried egg (1 per serving)

OPTIONAL TOPPING

Crushed seaweed

DIRECTIONS

1. Spray pan with avocado oil. Over medium heat, add chopped kimchi, and sauté for 2 to 3 minutes. Then add kale, tuna, hot pepper paste to taste, and chili flakes to pan. Sauté for another 2 to 3 minutes.

2. Lower heat, and add rice with kimchi juice. Mix well. Drizzle with sesame oil, and add sesame seeds.

3. To serve, top with a fried egg and crushed seaweed if desired.

ADD MORE KICK!

This dish has a little bit of a spicy kick, but it is still milder than the standard spicy kimchi fried rice. For grown-ups, you can always up the spice by adding more hot pepper paste and chili flakes.

SMALLER-BATCH NON-SPICY VERSION

🕐 TOTAL PREP/COOK TIME: 15 MINUTES

🥣 MAKES: 4 SERVINGS

INGREDIENTS

Avocado oil

½ cup rinsed and chopped kimchi

¼ cup finely chopped kale

3 oz canned tuna or salmon

2 cups cooked short-grain rice

1 tbsp low sodium soy sauce

½ tbsp sesame oil

1 tbsp sesame seeds

Fried egg (1 per serving)

DIRECTIONS

1. Spray pan with avocado oil. Over medium heat, sauté bite-sized pieces of kimchi for 2 to 3 minutes. Then add chopped kale, and sauté for another minute.

2. Add tuna or salmon to pan. Lower heat, and add cooked rice.

3. Add soy sauce and sesame oil. Sprinkle with sesame seeds.

4. Fry an egg in a separate pan, and add on top of fried rice when serving.

AIR FRYER CHICKEN KATSU WITH CABBAGE SALAD

If my daughter and son were asked what their favourite dinner is, no doubt this Chicken Katsu, a Japanese-style fried chicken cutlet, would be on their list. Actually, it would probably be on both my husband's and my list too. What's not to love? The best part is that it's made in an air fryer, so there is less mess, but the chicken is still juicy and crisp.

🕐 TOTAL PREP/COOK TIME: 25 MINUTES   🍲 MAKES: 4 SERVINGS

INGREDIENTS

2 large boneless chicken breasts (1.5 lb)

3 eggs

1 cup almond flour or all-purpose flour

1 tsp garlic powder

2 cups panko bread crumbs

Salt and pepper

Avocado oil

Shredded cabbage (desired amount as side salad)

DIRECTIONS

1. With a sharp knife, cut chicken breasts into thin cutlets by slicing horizontally into 2 pieces per breast. Place sliced chicken in a plastic bag, and pound with a meat mallet until about an even ¼ inch thickness. Season chicken cutlets with salt and pepper to taste.

2. Whisk 3 eggs in a shallow bowl. In another bowl, mix almond flour with garlic powder. Put 2 cups panko bread crumbs in a third bowl.

3. Dip each breast in flour, then eggs, and finally panko bread crumbs.

4. Spray air fryer and top of cutlets with a little avocado oil. Air fry at 350°F for 10 minutes. Flip cutlets over, and air fry for another 5 to 8 minutes.

OVEN METHOD

Preheat oven to 400°F. After steps 1 to 3, place cutlets on a parchment-lined sheet pan, and bake in the oven for about 13 minutes. Then flip and bake for another 13 minutes until fully cooked through and golden.

KID FRIENDLY TIP

Slice Chicken Katsu into strips, and let kids dip in tangy tonkatsu sauce. Serve with a side of cabbage salad with dressing drizzled on top. If your kids prefer a different vegetable, try shredded carrots instead with the same dressing drizzled on top.

Cabbage Salad Dressing

INGREDIENTS

2 tbsp
    mayonnaise

2 tbsp ketchup

1 tsp sesame oil

1 tsp honey

1 tsp lemon juice

DIRECTIONS

Whisk all dressing ingredients together well. Drizzle over a side of shredded cabbage. Recipe can be doubled, depending on the amount of cabbage used.

VEGETABLE LO MEIN NOODLES

(+ SHRIMP OPTION)

When people ask me if I make separate meals for my kids, the answer is no. We all eat the same thing, and I simply modify how I serve it. Sometimes, I serve a dish deconstructed, omit some spice, and make sure to cut food accordingly to avoid choking hazards. These kid-friendly noodles are an excellent and easy family-friendly recipe. And it satisfies that craving for Chinese takeout!

🕐 TOTAL PREP/COOK TIME: 20 MINUTES 🥣 MAKES: 5 SERVINGS

INGREDIENTS

1 package (10 oz) lo mein egg noodles

2 cups mixed chopped vegetables (e.g., green and purple cabbage, carrots, celery, mushrooms, bell peppers, broccoli, and frozen corn and peas)

½ tbsp avocado oil

Roasted sesame seeds for sprinkling

FOR THE NOODLE SAUCE

2 to 3 tbsp low sodium soy sauce

1 tbsp rice vinegar

1 tsp sesame oil

1 tbsp honey

1 clove garlic, minced

2 tsp oyster sauce

½ tsp minced ginger

DIRECTIONS

1. Cook lo mein noodles according to package instructions, about 4 minutes. Do not overcook. Drain and set aside.

2. Prepare the noodle sauce. Add the sauce ingredients to a jar with a tight lid, and shake well. Wash and chop the desired vegetables, and set aside.

3. In a large pan or wok, heat avocado oil and sauté all the vegetables except for the cabbage for about 3 minutes until translucent. Add cabbage to the vegetables, and sauté for another minute.

4. Finally, add the cooked noodles to the vegetable medley. Pour in the sauce, and toss with tongs. Sprinkle with sesame seeds, and serve right away.

SHRIMP VARIATION

Over low heat, toss 2 cloves garlic, minced, in ½ tablespoon avocado oil until fragrant. Increase heat to medium, and place 20 shrimp (about 1 lb), thawed if frozen, in the pan. Sprinkle with paprika, salt, and pepper to taste. Cook for about 2 to 3 minutes per side until cooked through and pink in colour. Add cooked shrimp to the cooked noodles and vegetables, pour in sauce, and toss. Sprinkle with sesame seeds.

LUNCHBOX TIP

Set a serving of noodles aside at dinner to pack in a lunchbox the next day. If your child has the option of warming up their food, pack in a separate container that is microwave-friendly, or put in a preheated thermos in the morning.

LEMON BROCCOLI PASTA

Here is one of our all-time classic weeknight meals that also doubles well as a lunch the next day. You can choose to add shrimp, salmon, canned tuna, or grilled chicken breast to this dish, depending on what you have on hand.

🕐 TOTAL PREP/COOK TIME: 20 MINUTES 🍲 MAKES: 4 SERVINGS

INGREDIENTS

2 cups uncooked pasta of choice

3 tbsp olive oil, divided

2 cloves garlic, minced

2 cups chopped broccoli

Juice from 1 lemon, divided
 (+ lemon zest for serving if desired)

Salt and pepper

½ cup grated Parmesan cheese
 (+ more for sprinkling on top)

¼ cup reserved pasta water

1 cup panko bread crumbs, toasted

NOTE

A kids-cut ABC pasta is fun, but penne and rigatoni also work well.

DIRECTIONS

1. Cook pasta in a pot of boiling water according to package instructions. Drain and set aside, reserving ¼ cup of cooking water.

2. Over low heat, in a large skillet or pot, sauté minced garlic in 2 tablespoons of oil until fragrant. Raise the heat to medium, add the chopped broccoli, and sauté for a few minutes more. Add half the lemon juice and salt and pepper to taste.

3. Add the pasta to the cooked garlic and broccoli. Add remaining olive oil, the rest of the lemon juice, and up to ¼ cup of reserved pasta water, depending on how dry the pasta feels. Add salt and pepper to taste. Stir together.

4. Lower heat, and add Parmesan cheese. Stir until the cheese melts.

5. To toast panko crumbs, heat in pan with a drizzle of olive oil over medium-low heat for 4 to 5 minutes. Stir frequently to prevent burning.

6. To serve, top with more grated Parmesan cheese, toasted panko bread crumbs, and a little lemon zest if desired.

LUNCHBOX TIP

To pack for lunch, heat up a thermos with hot water, letting water sit at least 5 minutes. Warm up pasta. Empty the water, add the hot pasta to the thermos, and seal with a lid. The pasta will stay warm until lunchtime. If desired, add cooked shrimp or salmon, canned tuna, or grilled chicken breast for added protein.

15-MINUTE PEANUT SESAME NOODLES

(+ GLUTEN-FREE OPTION)

Peanut sesame noodles are a great way to add the protein from peanut butter into your child's meals. These noodles are nutty, savoury, and subtly sweet. Top with some fresh cucumber matchsticks, sesame seeds, and extra crushed peanuts. Your whole family will be asking for more.

🕐 TOTAL PREP/COOK TIME: 15 MINUTES　🥄 MAKES: 4 TO 5 SERVINGS

INGREDIENTS

1 package (9 oz) thin udon or soba noodles

SAUCE

¼ cup all-natural peanut butter

2 tbsp low sodium soy sauce

2 tsp sesame oil (+ more for drizzling)

1 tbsp rice vinegar

1 tbsp honey

1 clove garlic, minced

¼ cup water

TOPPING

Sesame seeds

¼ cup cucumber matchsticks

¼ cup finely chopped peanuts

DIRECTIONS

1. Cook noodles according to package instructions. Do not overcook. Drain, rinse, and set aside.

2. In a separate saucepan, whisk the sauce ingredients together, and simmer over medium-low heat until well combined.

3. Stir sauce and noodles together. Drizzle sesame oil on top, and stir again.

4. Serve in bowls, and garnish with sesame seeds, fresh cucumber matchsticks, and crushed peanuts.

GLUTEN-FREE VARIATION

Use 100% buckwheat soba noodles, and replace soy sauce with coconut aminos.

KID FRIENDLY TIP

Try introducing beginner chopsticks to your kids when they are young. Using chopsticks will not only help with their fine motor skills and hand–eye coordination, but with all the fun design options available, it may also encourage your children to try new foods. Noodles are the perfect foods to eat with chopsticks.

ROOT VEGETABLE CURRY SOUP

(VEGAN)

My sister-in-law, Sarah, created this recipe and introduced it to us when visiting us in L.A. It's been a favourite ever since. The great thing about soups is that you can make a big batch in advance and have lots left over for the week, including for a hearty lunch. This soup is full of vegetables and chickpeas and is puréed down to a smooth flavourful soup that your kids will love. It's delicious and nutritious!

⏱ TOTAL PREP/COOK TIME: 45 MINUTES   🥄 MAKES: 8 TO 10 SERVINGS

INGREDIENTS

2 to 3 tbsp olive oil

1 cup diced onion

2 stalks celery, diced

2 to 3 cloves garlic, minced

1 tbsp minced fresh ginger

2 medium sweet potatoes, diced (4 cups)

1 medium butternut squash, diced (4 cups)

1 can (15 oz) chickpeas, drained and rinsed

1 tbsp curry powder

6 cups water

1 vegetable bouillon cube

1 can (13 oz) coconut milk

Salt and pepper

OPTIONAL TOPPING

Plain dairy-free yogurt

Croutons

DIRECTIONS

1. In a large pot or Dutch oven, sauté onion and celery in olive oil over medium heat until softened. Add garlic and ginger, and continue to sauté until translucent in colour. Add sweet potato and squash, and cook for approximately 5 minutes more. Stir in chickpeas.

2. Add curry powder, and continue to sauté for 5 more minutes, allowing the curry to toast.

3. Add 6 cups of water to mixture, bring to a boil, and add the vegetable bouillon cube. Stir to dissolve. Cover, and simmer over medium-low heat for 30 minutes or until vegetables are tender. Then remove from heat.

4. With a hand blender, blend until puréed. Pour in coconut milk until desired consistency is reached. Return to the burner, and heat through. Add salt and pepper to taste.

5. Serve with a dollop of dairy-free yogurt and/or croutons if desired.

LUNCHBOX TIP

My friend Kelly from @eattherainbow_kids introduced me to the fun and value of monochromatic lunchboxes. This lunchbox is all yellow, which can be a great way to add new inspiration to packing lunches. A monochromatic lunchbox can help you get more creative and push your own boundaries of what to buy, prepare, and serve. And, in turn, your children will naturally be exploring new foods, flavours, and textures as a result.

SLOW COOKER SPICY CHICKEN AND POTATO STEW

(DAKDORITANG)

In Korean, this dish is called *dakdoritang*. It's a delicious braised chicken and potato stew that's typically made in a pot. However, it tastes extra juicy and tender when cooked in a slow cooker — which takes the labour out of it too. This version has a bit of spice, but if you prefer a non-spicy version, just omit the red pepper paste and flakes. It tastes just as good. This was definitely one of my childhood favourites and is now one of my kids' favourites too.

🕐 PREP TIME: 5 MINUTES • TOTAL SLOW COOKER TIME: 6 TO 8 HOURS 🍲 MAKES: 4 SERVINGS

INGREDIENTS

1.5 lb skinless chicken drumsticks (about 6 drumsticks)

½ medium onion, chopped

2 cups baby potatoes, cut in half

1 cup baby carrots

1 cup water

Salt and pepper

1 cup chopped broccoli (optional)

Sesame seeds (topping)

SAUCE INGREDIENTS

3 cloves garlic, minced

1 tsp minced ginger

1 to 2 tbsp rice vinegar

¼ cup low sodium soy sauce

2 tsp Korean hot pepper paste (*gochujang*)

½ tsp Korean red chili flakes (*gochugaru*)

1 tbsp honey or maple syrup

1 tsp sesame oil

DIRECTIONS

1. Place drumsticks on the bottom of the slow cooker. Layer chopped onion, potato, and baby carrots on top. In a separate bowl, whisk sauce ingredients well, and pour over the chicken and vegetables, coating mixture well. Add 1 cup of water to the pot, season to taste with salt and pepper, and cover.

2. Turn the slow cooker to low, and cook for 6 to 8 hours until fully cooked through.

3. If adding broccoli, add 30 minutes before end of cooking.

4. Sprinkle finished dish with sesame seeds. Serve with a bowl of rice.

NOTE Just 5 minutes of prep in the morning — toss everything in a slow cooker — and dinner will be ready when you get home!

DESSERTS

Here you will find simple desserts, most consisting of only 5 ingredients that you and your kids can make together. From puff pastry to homemade ice pops and a delicious Korean-style shaved ice — there's something for everyone, with ingredients you probably already have at home.

Korean-Style Shaved
Ice With Fruit (p. 131)

GLAZED PEACH PUFF PASTRY TARTS

Puff pastry is versatile and extremely easy to work with. It is an ideal way to bake something quick and fun with your kids without a lot of mess. These puff pastry tarts are covered in thinly sliced peaches lightly sweetened with a little maple syrup. A scoop of vanilla ice cream is delicious on top!

⏱ TOTAL PREP/COOK TIME: 25 MINUTES   🍵 MAKES: 9 SQUARE SLICES

INGREDIENTS

1 sheet of store-bought puff pastry, thawed

1 large ripe peach, thinly sliced

Juice from ½ lemon

1 tbsp maple syrup (+ more for brushing on top)

½ tsp vanilla

OPTIONAL TOPPING

Powdered sugar

Vanilla ice cream

DIRECTIONS

1. Preheat oven to 400°F. Place sheet of puff pastry on a sheet pan (18 x 13 inches).

2. In a small bowl, mix the sliced peaches, lemon, and maple syrup together.

3. Layer the mixture on top of the puff pastry neatly in a line until covered.

4. Bake for 18 to 20 minutes until golden.

5. Let cool, and then slice into even square pieces. Brush a little maple syrup on top of the tarts. Sprinkle with powdered sugar if desired, or brush on a thin layer of simple glaze. Eat with a scoop of vanilla ice cream.

Simple Glaze

INGREDIENTS

¼ cup powdered sugar, sifted to remove lumps

2 ½ tsp water

½ tsp fresh lemon juice

DIRECTIONS

1. Combine the ingredients in a bowl, and whisk well.

2. With a pastry brush, brush a thin layer on top of the individual slices.

NOTE Store-bought puff pastry can be helpful in so many ways. It's nice to keep a package in your freezer for those days where you need a quick and easy snack or lunch idea. Kids love puff pastry!

KOREAN-STYLE SHAVED ICE WITH FRUIT

(+ DAIRY-FREE OPTION)

Summer holidays are no fun without a cool treat! A high-powered blender is best for this one, but a shaved ice maker would also work. This shaved ice is packed with summer fruits and sweetened with a little condensed milk. In Korea, it comes with sweet red beans, which you can add too, and it sometimes even comes topped with vanilla ice cream. This is meant to be shared and is a serving size for two.

🕐 PREP TIME: 10 MINUTES   🍴 MAKES: 2 SERVINGS

INGREDIENTS

A variety of desired amount of fruit (e.g., mango, peach, strawberries, cherries, honeydew melon, cantaloupe, red grapes, kiwi, pineapple, and watermelon)

4 cups ice

2 to 3 tbsp sweetened condensed milk

DIRECTIONS

1. Wash, chop, and dice desired fruit, and set aside.

2. Put ice in a high-powered blender, and blend on medium-high until ice is smooth with the consistency of snow.

3. Scoop shaved ice into a big bowl, and top with desired amount of diced fruit. Drizzle on condensed milk to taste. Mix gently with a spoon, or just eat as is.

DAIRY-FREE VARIATION

To make this dairy-free, replace the condensed milk with condensed oat milk or freshly squeezed juice.

KID FRIENDLY TIP

A scoop of ice cream or nice cream, tiny *mochi* (Japanese sweet rice dough) pieces, and chewy fruit snacks would be fun added touches in this too!

PEACH MANGO NICE CREAM

There are so many versions and flavours of nice cream, but this peach mango one is simple to make and has only a few ingredients. You can let your kids get really creative with their toppings for this quick and healthy cool, refreshing snack.

🕐 PREP TIME: 5 MINUTES
🍳 MAKES: 2 SERVINGS

INGREDIENTS

½ cup frozen peaches

½ cup frozen mangoes

1 ripe frozen banana

2 to 3 tbsp milk of choice or cream

Dash of vanilla extract (optional)

Chia seeds for sprinkling on top

OPTIONAL TOPPING

Granola, quinoa puffs, dye-free sprinkles

DIRECTIONS

1. Combine all ingredients except for the chia seeds in a high-powered blender or food processor, and process until smooth. The consistency should be like ice cream. (Do not add too much liquid, or it will turn into a smoothie consistency.)

2. Scoop and serve right away.

3. Sprinkle chia seeds on top for added nutrients and crunch. If desired, top with granola, quinoa puffs, and even dye-free sprinkles for a fun touch.

4. Store leftovers in the freezer.

MINI WATERMELON "CAKE"

The perfect summer fruit in my opinion is a sweet, juicy watermelon. And when watermelon is ripe and in season, it is the perfect dessert. Cut watermelon into rounds, and top the rounds with whipped cream and berries. This is a great way to celebrate summer holidays with minimal effort! My kids love this and will joyfully pick it up with their hands and eat it.

🕐 PREP TIME: 5 MINUTES

INGREDIENTS

Whole watermelon, cut into 2-inch slices

Strawberries (diced), blackberries, and blueberries

Whipped cream, store bought or homemade (p. 145)

DIRECTIONS

1. Using a fruit or cookie cutter, cut watermelon into desired shapes. Wash and prep strawberries, blackberries, and blueberries.

2. Pipe desired amount of whipped cream onto the watermelon cut-outs, and top with berries. Serve and eat right away!

COTTON CANDY GRAPE ICE POPS

If your kids love the taste of frozen grapes, this recipe is for them! These are especially great to make when grapes are in season and naturally sweet. This recipe calls for cotton candy grapes (the sweet white grapes that actually taste like cotton candy!) mixed with red grapes and frozen raspberries. Use fun ice-pop moulds to make them even more appealing, like the flamingo ones pictured here or little ring pop moulds.

🕐 PREP TIME: 5 MINUTES
FREEZE TIME: 6 HOURS TO OVERNIGHT
🥣 MAKES: 6 ICE POPS OR 16 RING ICE POPS

INGREDIENTS

1½ cups cotton candy grapes

1 cup red grapes

½ cup frozen raspberries

½ cup coconut water

DIRECTIONS

1. Combine all ingredients in a high-powered blender. Blend on medium speed for at least 30 seconds until smooth.

2. Pour the mixture through a fine mesh sieve (this will help remove the foam and extra fibres to create a smoother ice pop), and then pour into mould.

3. Place in the freezer for at least 6 to 8 hours or overnight.

4. When releasing the ice pop, slowly run under warm water, and then carefully pop it out.

LET'S CELEBRATE

Holidays and other special occasions are the perfect excuse to get creative with food. But with the busyness of the seasons, coupled with an overload of ideas and information, it's easy to get overwhelmed. So, my advice is to keep it simple.

In this section, you will find uncomplicated themed snack and lunch ideas, as well as traditional Korean dinner recipes that my family and I turn to again and again. Every family has its own traditions, and I am excited to share some of mine — inspired by the diverse influences in my family — for Lunar New Year, Valentine's Day, St. Patrick's Day, Halloween, Thanksgiving, Christmas, and birthdays.

LUNAR NEW YEAR

Lunar New Year is a traditional holiday celebrated by many different cultures. It's a time for families to gather together, cook and eat festive foods, wish for prosperity, and ring in the new year with joy and harmony. Here you will find three traditional Korean Lunar New Year recipes that are not only delicious but are also really popular with kids.

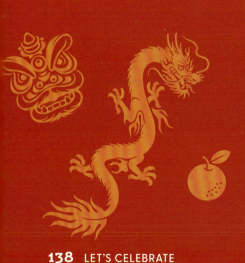

KOREAN RICE CAKE SOUP

(DDUK GUK)

Why do Koreans eat rice cake soup on New Year's Day? To celebrate health, longevity, wealth, and prosperity, of course. We keep up with the tradition every year. In fact, *dduk guk* is one of the first recipes my mother ever taught me. This recipe is a longer version that requires the beef brisket to simmer for at least two hours. There are also quicker, simpler versions without added beef and versions with an anchovy broth, but on New Year's Day, the slow simmer of beef brisket in a big pot is what's called for because it brings out the best flavour. *Dduk guk* is a favourite dish among many children I know, including mine!

🕐 TOTAL PREP/COOK TIME: 30 MINUTES • SIMMER TIME: 2 HOURS 🍲 MAKES: 5 TO 6 SERVINGS

INGREDIENTS

10 cups water

1 lb beef brisket

1 medium onion, whole

3 cloves garlic, peeled

2 pieces 2 x 3-inch *dashima* (dried kelp)

1 lb oval rice cakes

3 eggs (whites and yolks separated)

1 to 2 tbsp soup soy sauce

Salt and pepper

1 tsp sesame oil

FOR THE BEEF

1 tbsp low sodium soy sauce

1 tsp sesame oil

1 clove garlic, minced

TOPPING

Shredded marinated beef, sliced scallions, matchstick seaweed strips, sautéed carrot matchsticks, and egg white and yolk strips

DIRECTIONS

1. In a large Dutch oven or pot, bring water to a boil with beef, onion, garlic, and *dashima*. Remove *dashima* after 20 minutes. Let the stock simmer slowly, covered, for about 2 hours. Skim off any scum that may form at the top with a spoon.

2. If using frozen rice cakes, soak rice cakes in water for at least 10 minutes. Set aside.

3. Prepare the egg strips. Separate the egg whites and yolks. Mix whites together, and mix yolks together. In an oiled pan over medium-low heat, cook whites and yolks separately. Spread each egg mixture flat in the pan like a thin crepe. Once cooked, roll the cooked egg whites and the cooked egg yolks, and slice into thin strips. Set aside.

4. When beef has cooked for 2 hours, remove beef from the stock, and shred into small pieces. Add the beef ingredients (soy sauce, sesame oil, and minced garlic), and mix together. Set aside.

5. Remove the onion and garlic from the stock, and discard. Bring the stock to a rolling boil. Add the rice cakes and 1 to 2 tablespoons soup soy sauce to taste. Add salt and pepper to taste.

6. Let soup cook for another 5 minutes until rice cakes are soft and rise to the top. Drizzle soup with 1 teaspoon sesame oil. Serve rice cakes and soup in a bowl, and add the desired toppings.

MINI KOREAN-STYLE BEEF PATTIES

(DONGUERANG DDENG)

To celebrate Lunar New Year, it's traditional for Koreans to make all types of egg-battered appetizers like these savoury mini beef patties, also known as *donguerang ddeng* or *wanja-jeon*. They are quite simple to make but can be time-consuming since a large number tend to be prepared at a time. The reward, however, is the smile on your kids' faces as they devour them whole — not to mention all the extras in your freezer to save you on your busiest days.

🕐 TOTAL PREP/COOK TIME: 40 MINUTES 🍲 MAKES: 50 ROUND PATTIES

INGREDIENTS

1 lb ground beef (or ground pork, ground turkey/chicken, or a mixture)

1 package (14 oz) firm tofu, patted dry and crumbled

4 cloves garlic, minced

4 button mushrooms, finely diced

⅓ cup carrot, finely diced

½ medium onion, finely diced

2 green onions, finely sliced

1 tbsp sesame seeds

2 tbsp soy sauce

1 tbsp apple cider vinegar

1 tbsp sesame oil

1 tbsp sugar

Salt and pepper

3 heaping tbsp all-purpose flour

4 eggs, whisked

Avocado oil for the pan

DIRECTIONS

1. In a large mixing bowl, combine ground beef with tofu (crumble tofu well with your hands), garlic, mushrooms, carrots, onion, green onions, and sesame seeds. Using food-safe gloves, mix with your hands for at least 5 minutes, massaging and mixing until mixture is smooth.

2. In a separate jar or bowl, combine the soy sauce, apple cider vinegar, sesame oil, sugar, and black pepper. Whisk together. Then pour into the beef mixture. Add salt to taste.

3. Mix in flour last, and stir. (Alternatively, you can dredge patties in flour separately before dipping them in egg.) For each patty, scoop a tablespoon of the beef mixture, and form into a small round patty with your hands.

4. In a separate bowl, whisk eggs. (Add an additional clove of minced garlic to this egg mixture if you like more garlic.)

5. Scoop a teaspoon of the beef mixture, and form into a small round patty, about 1½ inches in diameter. Dip patties individually into the egg mixture, and place in a heated, oiled pan.

6. Pan-fry the patties for about 4 minutes per side over medium-low heat. Do not cook on high heat as you don't want the patties to burn. After cooking both sides, flip over again, pressing down slightly with a spatula. Make sure patties are cooked through before placing on a paper towel-lined plate.

7. Wipe pan in between batches to ensure a clean patty. Add more oil, and repeat the process with remaining patties.

FREEZER TIP

Place patties in a freezer-safe bag, and freeze for up to 3 months. Place in refrigerator to thaw, and reheat on a pan in the oven or microwave until fully heated through.

LUNCHBOX TIP

The patties are nice and compact, easy to eat with your hands, making them a popular lunchbox item. If your kids like to dip, pack with a side of ketchup or Tangy Soy Sauce Dip (p. 76). Reheat patties in the morning, and pack them in the lunchbox with rice, side veggies, and fruit.

EASY KOREAN GLASS NOODLES
(JAPCHAE NOODLES) (+ GLUTEN-FREE OPTION)

Noodles are a must for the Lunar New Year. To symbolize longevity, the longer the noodle the better. These glass noodles are not only long but are also slightly sweet and chewy. The ingredient list may seem lengthy, but once the vegetables and meat are all prepped, the cooking process is very easy. You can make adjustments with whatever vegetables you have on hand to have with the beef and a simple sauce. No need to wait for a special occasion; you can make this dish whenever you want. Kids love it!

🕐 TOTAL PREP/COOK TIME: 30 MINUTES • BEEF MARINATING TIME: 15 TO 30 MINUTES 🍳 MAKES: 6 SERVINGS

INGREDIENTS

6 oz sweet potato starch glass noodles

1 tsp avocado oil

3.5 oz beef sirloin, thinly sliced

1 small onion, thinly sliced

1 carrot, julienned

½ green bell pepper, thinly sliced

½ red bell pepper, thinly sliced

3 dried shitake mushrooms, presoaked and sliced

2 cloves garlic, minced

¾ cup water

3 tbsp soy sauce, divided

1 to 2 tbsp sugar or honey

2 cups baby spinach

1 green onion, sliced

Black pepper

2 tsp sesame oil

2 tbsp sesame seeds

DIRECTIONS

1. Boil the sweet potato starch noodles for 5 minutes. Rinse and then drain. Add 1 teaspoon of avocado oil to the noodles, mix, and set aside.

2. Prepare marinade for beef (see Sirloin Beef Marinade, p. 79) or use Quick Beef Marinade (following page). Let beef marinate for at least 15 to 30 minutes.

3. Sauté marinated beef in a heated, oiled pan over medium heat for about a minute, until browned. Add the onion, carrot, bell pepper, mushrooms, and garlic, and sauté for another few minutes. Remove the meat and vegetables from the pan, and set aside.

4. In the same pan, add the cooked noodles with ¾ cup of water, 2 tablespoons soy sauce, and 1 tablespoon sugar. Add the spinach and green onions. Keep stirring frequently until the liquid dissolves and the spinach is wilted (about 4 to 5 minutes).

5. Add the meat and vegetables that were set aside to the noodle mixture. Add the remaining 1 tablespoon of soy sauce. Add 1 more tablespoon of sugar if desired. Season with black pepper to taste. Finally, add 2 teaspoons sesame oil and 2 tablespoons sesame seeds. Mix together and serve.

VARIATION

Sweet potato starch noodles are gluten-free. To make this dish completely gluten-free, substitute coconut aminos for the soy sauce.

Quick Beef Marinade

INGREDIENTS

2 cloves garlic, minced

½ tbsp soy sauce

1 tsp sesame oil

2 tsp honey

¼ tsp black pepper

DIRECTIONS

1. Combine the ingredients in a bowl, and whisk well.

2. Pour sauce over beef and let marinate.

NOTE *Japchae* noodles taste great the next day as the flavours get to blend. Try adding the noodles to a bowl of rice, and mix together to make *japchae bap* (rice) This is another favourite for kids and makes a great lunchbox idea too. Pack in a thermos to keep it warm.

VALENTINE'S DAY

Heart season is the best season in my opinion! Maybe it's just me, but I think everything looks and tastes better when shaped like a heart. All you need is a few different-sized heart-shaped cookie and fruit and vegetable cutters, and just like that, your children's interest will be piqued.

Share a fun Valentine's Day moment with your kids, and make these easy heart-shaped strawberry shortcake puff pastries. Cut strawberries into hearts, and put them on a lollipop stick. And make a festive, kid-friendly sweet and savoury charcuterie board for your next Valentine's Day party.

HEART-SHAPED STRAWBERRY SHORTCAKE PUFF PASTRIES

These heart-shaped strawberry shortcake puff pastries, sweetened with just a little maple syrup, are my kids' favourite dessert. The flaky crust and pillowy whipped cream will have you longing for more. And when heart season is over, you can opt for an even quicker and easier version and make these into 8 even squares instead.

⏱ TOTAL PREP/COOK TIME: 20 MINUTES 🥄 MAKES: 7 HEARTS OR 8 SQUARES

INGREDIENTS

1 sheet of store-bought puff pastry

Flour for dusting

1 cup diced strawberries

1 tbsp lemon juice

1 cup heavy whipping cream

1½ tbsp maple syrup, divided

1 egg, beaten

OPTIONAL TOPPING

Powdered sugar

NOTE Save all the excess strawberry bits in a freezer-safe bag to use for smoothies so that there is zero waste!

DIRECTIONS

1. Preheat oven to 400°F. Thaw puff pastry according to package instructions. Dust clean surface with a little flour, and lay out thawed puff pastry.

2. Using a medium-sized heart-shaped cookie cutter, cut out 7 hearts. (Alternatively, use a pizza cutter and cut 8 squares.) Use a pastry brush to brush each shape with beaten egg.

3. Place on a parchment-lined sheet pan 2 inches apart, and bake for 10 to 12 minutes.

FOR THE STRAWBERRIES

Mix diced strawberries with lemon juice and ½ tablespoon of maple syrup. Set aside.

FOR THE WHIPPED CREAM

Using a handheld blender with the whisk attachment, whip 1 cup of heavy cream with 1 tbsp of maple syrup until soft peaks form. Do not over-whisk.

TO ASSEMBLE

1. Using a sharp knife, slice a small hole or opening on the side of the heart puff pastry.

2. Carefully fill each heart with 1 to 2 teaspoons of strawberries. Then pipe in whipped cream. (If you don't have a piping bag, you can fill a plastic bag with whipped cream, cut a small hole at the corner, and pipe the whipped cream that way.)

3. Dust with a little powdered sugar on top if you wish.

Strawberry Hearts on a Stick

In keeping with February's theme, try cutting strawberries into a heart shape and sticking them through a lollipop stick. You will be surprised at how this simple change will light up your children's faces. I mean, it's practically a lollipop!

DIRECTIONS

1. Cut a large strawberry in half lengthwise.

2. Place a heart cutter (1½ inch x 1½ inch) on top, press down, and remove excess strawberry.

3. Slide strawberry heart onto a lollipop stick. Repeat and layer so that there are three strawberry hearts on a stick.

KID-FRIENDLY VALENTINE CHARCUTERIE BOARD

When building a charcuterie board for kids, start with the basics first. You will need cheese, preferably a couple of different kinds, crackers, fruit, and veggies. Heart-shaped crackers are fun for Valentine's Day as are heart-shaped ramekins to fill with dips or fruit. The best part of building a charcuterie board is looking around your grocery store and finding fun and interesting new snacks to fill it.

ON THIS BOARD

Heart-shaped crackers

Sharp cheddar cheese, sliced

Babybel cheese

Camembert cheese

Mini cornichons

Red pepper jelly (fig jam and apricot jam are also good)

Mandarins, peeled and sliced

Cherry tomatoes (halved or quartered)

Celery and baby carrots, sliced

Dye-free candy-coated chocolate pieces

Salami (nitrite/nitrate free) or roasted turkey slices

DIRECTIONS

1. Start by placing the ramekins on a clean wooden board. Fill these with dips or anything liquid-based. Small ramekins are good for holding jams. Add a little spoon for scooping.

2. Place the Camembert cheese in the middle, and neatly layer the folded salami around it. Then layer the crackers. Place the other cheeses. Arrange the baby carrots and celery slices around the edge, along with the other vegetables, mandarins, and cornichons.

3. Fill the holes with some dye-free candy-coated chocolate.

NOTE For the Babybel cheese, use a heart-shaped fruit cutter (1 inch x 1 inch) to cut out the shape right on the wax. Press down and pull.

KID FRIENDLY TIP For parties and get-togethers, you can also make individual charcuterie plates. This way, each child can have their own plate already made. You can use little bamboo skewers to hold fruit and cheese together for easy handling.

My husband's side of the family is Irish, so naturally we like to celebrate St. Patrick's Day with rainbows and something green for the kids! Traditionally, my mother-in-law makes corned beef and cabbage and Irish soda bread. We all wear something green to mark the occasion.

RAINBOW PIZZA

For an easy St. Patrick's Day–themed lunch, a rainbow pizza is fun. Make it on garlic naan or pita bread for ease!

🕐 TOTAL PREP/COOK TIME: 15 MINUTES 🍲 MAKES: 4 PIECES

Rainbow Naan Pizza

INGREDIENTS

½ cup pizza or marinara sauce

1 cup shredded mozzarella cheese

4 pieces garlic naan or pita bread

TOPPINGS OF CHOICE

(e.g., green, red, yellow, orange bell peppers, purple onions, mushrooms)

DIRECTIONS

1. Preheat oven to 400°F. Spread pizza sauce on top of garlic naan, and top with shredded cheese. Place desired toppings with all the colours of the rainbow.

2. Bake for 9 to 11 minutes, or air fry at 330°F for 7 minutes.

Pizza makes a great lunchbox item.

KID
FRIENDLY
T I P

Another fun St. Patrick's Day idea is to make our Green Smoothie (p. 52). Serve it in a tall rainbow glass. Top with a dollop of honey yogurt and fun, dye-free, green sprinkles.

HALLOWEEN

Halloween is one of our favourite times of the year. It is one of the best times to step out of your comfort zone and really get creative with your food. In this section, I have everything from breakfasts and snacks to lunchbox ideas and a no-fuss dinner platter idea to inspire your next Halloween party — or simply a fun Halloween with your kids.

KID
FRIENDLY
T I P

For Halloween parties, prepare fruit salad in decorative individual cups with little spoons or food picks. Place them on the buffet table for an easy treat kids can grab themselves.

HALLOWEEN FRUIT SALAD

Fruit salad is so easy to make and great to prep in advance! Use Halloween colours to make it festive and a mushroom-shaped fruit and vegetable cutter to mimic the look of a skeleton head. Top if off with candied googly eyes.

⏱ PREP TIME: 15 MINUTES 🍲 MAKES: 4 SERVINGS

INGREDIENTS

1 apple, washed and peeled

½ cup blackberries

½ cup blueberries

½ cup pomegranate seeds

2 mandarin oranges, peeled

Juice from ½ orange

1 tbsp maple syrup

Mint leaf for garnish

DIRECTIONS

1. Wash the berries. Slice apples into thin slices, and then use a small mushroom-shaped fruit and vegetable cutter to cut out shapes. Combine the apple and the rest of the fruit in a medium mixing bowl.

2. Add juice from the orange, and mix together. Then add maple syrup, and mix again until well combined. Garnish with a mint leaf.

LUNCHBOX TIP

Fruit salad offers a good variety and works really well in a school lunchbox. It's also easy to prepare ahead of time. Just make sure to pack it in a leakproof container.

MONSTER CHOCOLATE CHIP BANANA MUFFINS

How can you make green muffins appetizing to a kid? Make them into ghoulish monsters for Halloween, of course! This is our favourite chocolate chip banana muffin recipe, and we just added a little spinach to make it green. I promise you, you and your kids won't even be able to taste the spinach!

⏱ TOTAL PREP/COOK TIME: 30 MINUTES 🥄 MAKES: 12 MUFFINS

INGREDIENTS

1 cup all-purpose flour

½ cup almond flour

1 tsp baking powder

1 tsp baking soda

Pinch of salt

1 tsp cinnamon

3 ripe bananas

½ cup spinach

¼ cup unsweetened almond milk

¼ cup butter, melted

¼ cup cane sugar or maple syrup

1 egg, lightly beaten

¼ cup chocolate chips (+ extra to melt for the decoration on top)

Candy googly eyes for decoration

DIRECTIONS

1. Preheat oven to 350°F. Mix together the dry ingredients in a mixing bowl. Mash bananas in another bowl. Combine spinach and milk in a blender, and blend until smooth. Add spinach and milk mixture to the bananas, along with the melted butter, sugar, and egg.

2. Add the wet mixture to the dry ingredients, and mix. Stir in ¼ cup chocolate chips.

3. Grease a muffin tin or use muffin liners, and fill cups with batter ¾ full. Bake for 20 to 23 minutes until a toothpick inserted comes out clean.

FOR THE MONSTER FACE

Heat chocolate chips in the microwave in 15-second intervals until melted. Place in a small piping or plastic bag with a tiny slit cut in the corner, and pipe the design right on top of the muffin. Place 2 candy googly eyes on top, securing them with a bit of chocolate. A small piping tip would be helpful if you would like to make the design more intricate.

KID FRIENDLY TIP Present your kids with the tools, and then let them decorate the muffins themselves. Watch their creativity shine!

HALLOWEEN BREAKFAST BOARD

I must admit, I have an extensive collection of waffle makers that make fun shapes for every occasion. These pumpkin and spiderweb waffles come out every year, but if you don't have one of these, just use a regular waffle maker. Pancakes would also be a good alternative. Place everything on a big breakfast platter for a fun communal Halloween family breakfast.

ON THIS BOARD

Pumpkin waffles

Hard-boiled eggs

Sliced persimmon, cut into pumpkin shapes

Pink dragon fruit

Bacon

Raspberries

Blackberries

Greek yogurt (chocolate chips as the eyes and mouth)

DIRECTIONS

1. Make pumpkin waffles.

2. Use silicone liners to hold the yogurt and any other wet foods in place. Place in the centre of a serving platter or board.

3. Layer waffles around the sides, along with the bacon and eggs. Fill in any holes with more fruit. Use Halloween-themed food picks in the fruit for easy handling.

Pumpkin Waffles

DIRECTIONS

1. Add ¼ to ⅓ cup of pumpkin purée and ½ teaspoon of pumpkin spice to ¾ cup of your favourite pancake mix. Stir in ½ cup of water.

2. Makes 6 waffles.

NOTE

Use a store-bought mix when time is limited. Mixes can be adapted quite easily. In this recipe, I added pumpkin purée to the mix. You can also add nutritional boosts with vegetables, fruit, and seeds.

HALLOWEEN MUFFIN-TIN SNACK TRAY

Halloween night can be bustling with energy and excitement, and sometimes, a simple, no-fuss platter dinner is what's called for. Make it fun, balanced, filling, and not too complicated. Here, I prepared easy chicken nuggets, crackers and cheese, guacamole, and a variety of fruit and vegetables. Add some fun by adding candied or blueberry eyeballs.

ON THIS PLATTER

Crackers and cheddar cheese, cut into pumpkin shapes

Chicken nuggets with ketchup

Guacamole with ghost-shaped chips

Carrot ghosts and celery with peanut butter (add googly eyes)

Blueberry eyeballs with white chocolate chips

Pomegranate skeleton head with blueberry white chocolate chip eyeballs

DIRECTIONS

1. Use a fun muffin-tin tray or a skeleton-shaped tray like this one as the serving platter.

2. Cut out pumpkin shapes on cheddar cheese slices with a pumpkin-shaped cutter. Pair with crackers.

3. Add a protein. Here we have chicken nuggets with ketchup.

4. Add guacamole and chips. Put some pomegranate seeds on top of the guacamole for extra colour.

5. Use a small metal straw to poke out holes on the crinkle-cut carrot slices to make them into ghosts.

6. Put peanut butter on celery, and add a candied eyeball.

7. Stick white chocolate chips or yogurt chips into blueberries to make eyeballs.

8. Add eyeballs on top of a scoop of pomegranate seeds for the Halloween theme.

SIMPLE HALLOWEEN LUNCH INSPIRATION

If Halloween lands on a school day, here are some fun and simple ways to make lunch a little more festive. Sandwich cutters are the easiest method to create simple food art. It takes only an extra minute of your time and will completely change up the vibe of your kids' lunchbox.

LUNCHBOX ONE

Oven-roasted turkey slices with cheddar cheese on whole wheat bread cut into a spiderweb. Add mustard, mayonnaise, and lettuce if desired. Halloween pretzels. Blueberry and grape skewers with yogurt dip and dye-free Halloween-coloured sprinkles. Mini orange bell pepper with cream cheese and googly eyes. Crinkle-cut carrots.

LUNCHBOX TWO

Ham and Gruyère cheese on whole wheat bread cut into a jack-o'-lantern. Add mayonnaise and sliced cornichon pickles. Halloween ghost-shaped chips. Moondrop grapes a.k.a. witch fingers with sliced almonds as the fingertip. Broccoli and celery with ranch dressing. And a pumpkin gummy drop.

WITCHES BROOMS

As a Korean Canadian living in America, I celebrate three Thanksgivings! In Korean, Thanksgiving is called *Chuseok*. It is a time for us to honour our ancestors and to reflect, give thanks, and gather together with ample amounts of traditional food. Popular foods we eat are different types of *jeon*, which are Korean pancakes (p. 76), and egg-battered appetizers, like Korean-Style Beef Patties (p. 140), which are also made at Lunar New Year, rice cakes, and fruit. You will find a favourite Korean Egg-Battered Cod (p. 160) recipe in this section, along with my mother-in-law's famous Flaky Buttermilk Pumpkin Biscuits on this page and a delightful and easy dessert, Chocolate-Dipped Persimmons (p. 162).

FLAKY BUTTERMILK PUMPKIN BISCUITS

This pumpkin biscuit recipe was passed down to me from my mother-in-law, and we make these every Thanksgiving because the biscuits are a big hit with the kids. Who knew baking biscuits from scratch would be so easy? You can whip these up in no time, and you probably have all of the ingredients already in your pantry.

🕐 TOTAL PREP/COOK TIME: 30 MINUTES
🍲 MAKES: 8 LARGE BISCUITS OR 12 MINI BISCUITS

INGREDIENTS

1 cup all-purpose flour	½ tsp salt
¾ cup spelt flour	½ cup cold butter
2 tbsp brown sugar	½ cup buttermilk
2 tsp baking powder	¾ cup pumpkin purée
1 tsp baking soda	

DIRECTIONS

1. Preheat oven to 425°F. In a large mixing bowl, combine flours, brown sugar, baking powder, baking soda, and salt. With a pastry blender, cut in butter until the mixture looks like coarse crumbs. (If you don't have a pastry blender, you can use 2 butter knives, and cut the butter into pea-sized amounts.)

2. Add the buttermilk and pumpkin purée to the dry mixture, and stir just until moistened.

3. On a floured surface, knead mixture about 8 times. Do not over-knead. Roll out the dough to a 1-inch thickness. Cut out with a 3-inch-round cookie cutter (use a 2-inch cookie cutter for mini biscuits).

4. Place on a greased baking sheet or parchment-lined baking sheet one inch apart. For large biscuits, bake for 16 to 18 minutes or until golden brown. For smaller biscuits, bake for 12 to 14 minutes.

KID FRIENDLY TIP

Sometimes a big plate of food at Thanksgiving can be overwhelming for children. It helps not to overload a plate. You can start with a small amount of food and give children more when they ask for more. Use a divided plate so that food can be neatly organized. Add a mini biscuit on the side as their one food that you know they love. Both my kids, the younger one and the older one, always go for the biscuit first.

NOTE You can make these biscuits in big batches and then freeze them for quick and easy lunches and meals to be ready whenever you need them. Just store them in a freezer-friendly bag for up to 3 months, let thaw, and reheat in a pan. Simple and delicious!

EGG-BATTERED COD

(SAENG SUN JEON)

This Korean egg-battered fish dish is inspired by my mother's cooking. So many times I've seen my mother making versions of this Korean appetizer – some with beef, oysters, shrimp, and my personal favourite, white fish. This super simple recipe is a Korean staple for occasions like Korean Thanksgiving (*Chuseok*), but the fish also makes a great lunchbox addition for every day! Not only is this recipe delicious, but there are also just a few simple ingredients. This is one of the easiest and quickest dishes to make.

⏱ TOTAL PREP/COOK TIME: 15 TO 20 MINUTES   🍲 MAKES: 15 PIECES (APPROXIMATELY)

INGREDIENTS

1 lb cod

Salt and pepper

2 eggs

¾ cup almond flour or all-purpose flour

1 tsp garlic powder

1 tbsp avocado oil

DIRECTIONS

1. With a paper towel, blot fish to remove excess water. With a sharp knife, slice fish with the grain on a diagonal into thin slices, a little thinner than ½ inch if possible. Season both sides with salt and pepper to taste.

2. Whisk eggs together. In a separate bowl, combine flour and garlic powder. Dredge the fish in the flour first and then the egg.

3. Heat avocado oil in a pan over medium-low heat. Pan-fry battered cod for 2 to 3 minutes per side until fully cooked through.

NOTE

Make sure not to have the heat too high; otherwise, the egg batter will be too browned.

KID FRIENDLY TIP

We ran out of oil one day and pan-fried these with a little butter and the taste was – well – buttery and incredible! And the kids loved them.

CHOCOLATE-DIPPED PERSIMMONS

The easiest and most delicious way to serve dessert is to dip fruit into chocolate. Strawberries, mandarins, and kiwi are great options, but so are persimmons! This popular Asian fruit comes out every fall/winter, so it's the perfect dessert to celebrate fall harvest and *Chuseok* celebrations. In Korean, we call this fruit *gam* and eat it just like an apple with or without skin. Both ways are really good.

🕐 TOTAL PREP/COOK TIME: 5 MINUTES • CHOCOLATE HARDENING TIME: 20 MINUTES TO 1 HOUR
🥄 MAKES: 10 CHOCOLATE-DIPPED PERSIMMON SLICES

INGREDIENTS

2 to 3 persimmons (non-astringent variety)

1 cup dark or milk chocolate chips

1 tsp coconut oil

Dye-free sprinkles

NOTE This technique also works with many other fruits, including strawberries, kiwi, and mandarin oranges. If time is short, this is a great last-minute dessert to present for your kids' fall festivity parties.

DIRECTIONS

1. Wash and thinly slice persimmons, discarding the top stem.

2. Melt chocolate chips and coconut oil in a microwave-safe bowl in 15-second intervals until melted, stirring in between. (You can also use the double-boiler method on a stove.)

3. Dip half of each sliced persimmon into the chocolate, and lay it down on parchment paper. Sprinkle on desired quantity of sprinkles.

4. Let chocolate harden for at least 20 minutes to 1 hour in the refrigerator, and then enjoy!

CHRISTMAS

There's nothing better than getting into the Christmas spirit with festive food and colours. In this section, you will find the best Chewy Ginger Molasses Cookies (p. 165), which can double as gingerbread people cookies, a simple but effective Avocado Sushi Wreath (p. 166) and Tofu Miso Soup (p. 167), along with a cute Christmas Tree Snack Board (p. 169) for kids, which can easily be made for play dates and Christmas get-togethers.

CHEWY GINGER MOLASSES COOKIES

It wasn't until I met my husband that I was introduced to the sweet aroma of Christmas cookies baking in the oven. If you're looking for a must-make Christmas cookie, this chewy ginger cookie is it. My sister-in-law makes these cookies every Christmas and we look forward to them every year. Of course, on occasions when we can't visit, I have to make the recipe myself to nurture that "home at Christmas" craving.

The best thing about this recipe is that the same dough works to make gingerbread people too, which is always fun for the kids to help make.

🕐 TOTAL PREP/COOK TIME: 20 MINUTES
• CHILLING TIME: 30 MINUTES 🥄 MAKES: 24 COOKIES (2-INCH DIAMETER)

INGREDIENTS

½ cup butter, softened	1 cup whole wheat flour
½ cup raw cane sugar	2 tsp baking soda
¼ cup brown sugar	1½ tsp ground ginger
1 egg	1 tsp cinnamon
¼ cup blackstrap molasses	Pinch of salt
1 cup all-purpose flour	Sugar for dipping

DIRECTIONS

1. Cream butter and sugar with a hand mixer in a large mixing bowl until fluffy. Mix in egg, and then add the molasses. In a separate bowl, mix the dry ingredients (except for sugar for dipping) together. Slowly add the dry ingredients to the wet ingredients, and mix on low speed until combined.

2. Cover and chill the dough in the refrigerator for at least 30 minutes or up to 24 hours.

3. Preheat oven to 350°F. Remove dough from the refrigerator. Using a small cookie scoop, roll dough into small balls, and dip one side into sugar. Cookies should be 2 inches in diameter when baked. Place on a parchment-lined cookie sheet sugar side up.

4. Bake for 8 to 10 minutes until brown and crinkly. Do not overbake. Transfer to a cooling rack, and let cool for about 5 minutes.

Christmas Gingerbread People Cookies

🥄 MAKES: 10 COOKIES

Follow the same ingredient list (omit sugar for dipping) and complete step 1. Once the ingredients are combined, flatten dough into a round circle, and wrap in plastic wrap. Cover and chill dough for at least 1 to 2 hours or overnight. Carefully roll out the dough to about ¼ inch thickness, and cut out shapes with a cookie cutter. I use a 3 x 2-inch cookie cutter. Gently roll out the remaining dough, and repeat. Place on a parchment-lined cookie sheet, and bake for 9 to 11 minutes at 350°F. Once cooled, let your kids use their creativity and ice the cookies with cookie icing using a small piping tip.

AVOCADO SUSHI WREATH

When I was growing up, my parents would often order a big platter of sushi for Christmas Day. It was a fun tradition. We would eat midday before our big Christmas dinner — and yes, we always had room to eat more. When I got married, my parents continued this tradition and brought over a big platter of sushi to my in-laws' house. We ate and bonded and clinked our glasses to the New Year.

Here is an easy, kid-friendly cucumber avocado roll that we make into a fun Christmas wreath to be extra festive.

🕐 PREP TIME: 15 MINUTES   🥄 MAKES: 2 ROLLS (10 PIECES PER ROLL)

INGREDIENTS

1 cup cooked white or brown sushi rice, cooled

½ tsp rice vinegar

½ tbsp sesame seeds

Salt

2 sheets unsalted roasted seaweed

½ avocado, peeled and sliced

Squeeze of Kewpie mayonnaise per roll (optional)

DIRECTIONS

1. Add rice vinegar, sesame seeds, and salt to taste to cooled rice and mix.

2. Lay the roasted seaweed flat on top of a sushi rolling mat, shiny side down. Spread rice evenly on the seaweed only halfway. Wet fingers to mash rice down so that it doesn't stick to your hand. Layer the sliced avocado on top. Squeeze a thin line of mayonnaise on top from one end to the other.

3. Take both the rolling mat and seaweed, and start rolling tightly until it gets to the end. Seal the end with a little bit of water with your fingertip (like sealing an envelope).

4. With a sharp knife, slice thinly into rolls. Wet your knife a little to avoid sticking in between each slice.

5. To make the wreath, place the rolls on a plate in a circle. Add a cluster of raspberries at the top and matchstick carrots to make a bow. Serve with a side of Tofu Miso Soup (following page).

Tofu Miso Soup

⏱ TOTAL PREP/COOK TIME: 15 MINUTES 🍚 MAKES: 2 SERVINGS

INGREDIENTS

2 ½ cups water

1 square 3-inch piece *kombu* (dried kelp)

2 tbsp miso paste

⅓ block (6 oz) tofu, cut into small cubes

¼ cup chopped spinach

Thinly sliced scallions for garnish

DIRECTIONS

1. In a small pot, bring water to a boil, and add dried kelp. Lower heat, cover, and let simmer for 10 minutes; then remove and discard the dried kelp.

2. Add miso paste to broth. Add cubed tofu and spinach. Let simmer together for a few more minutes.

3. Serve with thinly sliced scallions on top.

NOTE When adding miso paste, it helps to put the paste in a ladle and add some broth to it. Press down on the miso with the back of a spoon a few times, and let it dissolve before adding to the rest of the broth.

KID FRIENDLY TIP When my daughter was a picky toddler, I started adding small amounts of chopped spinach or kale into our miso soup to squeeze in an extra veggie. I was surprised that she was eating it without hesitation. The beauty of miso soup is that you can't even taste the spinach. The flavourful miso and spinach go well together.

Avocado Cucumber Rolls Inside Out

If the rice, cucumber, and avocado are already prepared from the night before, the rolls can easily be assembled in the morning. To make these rolls inside out, simply flip the seaweed with the rice covering one side over so that the rice is now facing down on the bamboo mat. Add cucumber and avocado with Kewpie mayonnaise on the seaweed side, and begin rolling upward starting from the bottom. Slice with a wet, sharp knife.

CHRISTMAS TREE SNACK BOARD

Snack boards are the easiest way to accommodate a group of kids, whether it's a small gathering or a simple play date. Make this Christmas tree snack board for your next holiday get-together, and impress the adults and the kids alike. No one will know how easy it was to actually create.

⏲ PREP TIME: 15 MINUTES   🥣 MAKES: 1 SNACK BOARD

DIRECTIONS

1. On a wooden board, start by decorating the top of the "tree." Spread nut butter and strawberry or raspberry jam on whole wheat bread, and cut out a star-shaped sandwich. With a smaller star cookie cutter, cut out the middle of the other slice of bread so that the jam is peeking through.

2. Layer in tree formation from the top: sliced cucumbers, sliced cheddar cheese, Christmas tree- or star-shaped crackers, peanut butter and jam roll-ups, mandarin oranges, raspberries, crinkle-cut avocado, and some pomegranate seeds on top of the cucumbers as extra "ornament" decoration.

Peanut Butter and Jam Roll-Ups

DIRECTIONS

Cut crusts off soft whole wheat bread, and roll slices with a rolling pin until flat. Spread peanut butter and jam on top. Roll from one end tightly, and then slice into small pieces.

BIRTHDAY

Surprise friends, family, and your kids with these cute and compact Korean-style lunchbox cakes. There are endless creative ways to decorate them, making it easy to customize for your little ones and friends. Add a note and a candle to the top of the lid, and make it a special delivery. Also included in this section is a traditional Korean seaweed soup that my mom made for me on every birthday. I used to just call it birthday soup! It is so easy to make, however, that it's really a soup for every day.

KOREAN-STYLE LUNCHBOX CAKE

Korean-style lunchbox cakes are minimal and petite, packaged neatly in a takeout container. They make the perfect gift for special occasions, and I love that they are easy to make and pack. Line the takeout container with decorative parchment paper, and make sure to add your own touch of whimsy. We love this sponge cake because it's so fluffy and light and has the perfect balance of sweetness, but if time is limited, you can use a boxed cake mix.

🕐 PREP TIME: 10 MINUTES
• BAKE TIME: 25 MINUTES
🍚 MAKES: TWO 4-INCH DOUBLE-LAYERED CAKES

INGREDIENTS

1 cup cake flour

1½ tsp baking powder

Pinch of salt

4 eggs, whites and yolks, separated

¼ cup milk of choice

1½ tsp vanilla extract

¼ cup avocado oil

¾ cup sugar

½ tsp lemon juice

DIRECTIONS

1. Preheat oven to 350°F.

2. Sift flour, baking powder, and salt into a large mixing bowl.

3. Add milk, vanilla, and oil to the egg yolks.

4. In a separate bowl, add sugar to the egg whites, and whip with a stand mixer or hand mixer until frothy. Add lemon juice. Whip until stiff peaks form.

5. Add dry ingredients to wet ingredients, and mix. Gently fold in the whipped egg whites.

6. Line a 9 x 13-inch pan with parchment paper. Grease. Pour in batter, and bake for approximately 25 minutes or until a toothpick comes out clean.

7. Once baked and cooled, use a 4-inch round cake cutter to cut out 4 circles. Each cake will use two pieces to create a double layer cake. Level the cakes with a knife to make them even, and frost in between the layers. You can add fruit in between the layers, as well, such as sliced strawberries, kiwi, peaches, grapes, and blueberries. Use an icing spatula to apply icing to the entire cake, and decorate as you wish.

Chocolate Whipped Cream Frosting

This frosting is my go-to frosting because it is so simple and can be made in under 5 minutes. It gives a subtle hint of cocoa and has a perfect "not-too-sweet" quality.

INGREDIENTS

1 cup heavy whipping cream

1 tsp cocoa powder

1 to 2 tbsp powdered sugar

DIRECTIONS

Combine all ingredients in a large mixing bowl. Whip with the whisk attachment on a hand mixer until stiff peaks form. Refrigerate once the cake is decorated with this frosting.

Strawberry Buttercream Frosting

INGREDIENTS

8 tbsp butter, softened

½ tsp vanilla extract

2 to 3 tsp milk of choice

1½ cups powdered sugar

⅓ cup freeze-dried strawberries, finely ground

DIRECTIONS

With a hand or stand mixer, beat butter on medium speed for about 2 minutes. Then add the vanilla extract, milk, powdered sugar, and freeze-dried strawberries. Beat 2 more minutes or until frosting is nice and creamy. Add more milk until frosting is the desired consistency.

KOREAN SEAWEED SOUP

(MIYEOK GUK)

Traditionally, Koreans eat seaweed soup (*miyeok guk*) on their birthday because of its association with birth. My mother made me variations of this soup for an entire month after I gave birth to both my kids to help with my recovery. You would think I would be sick of it, but no. It's still one of my favourite soups — especially since it's so easy to make with a few simple ingredients! And my kids enjoy it not only on their birthday but regularly as well.

⏱ TOTAL PREP/COOK TIME: 35 MINUTES   🍲 MAKES: 8 SERVINGS

INGREDIENTS

0.5 oz dried seaweed (*miyeok*)

5 oz stewing beef

2 tsp sesame oil

1 to 2 cloves garlic, minced (optional)

1½ tbsp soup soy sauce (*guk ganjang*), divided

6 cups water

Salt and pepper

DIRECTIONS

1. Place seaweed in a bowl with enough water to cover the seaweed. Let it soak for at least 10 minutes. Then drain and rinse well. (The seaweed will expand.) Slice beef into small, thin pieces, and sprinkle with salt and pepper to taste. (I like to be more generous with the pepper.) Set aside.

2. In a large pot or Dutch oven, sear the meat with the sesame oil for about 1 minute over medium-high heat. Lower heat, and add minced garlic with the meat if you like. Add the rinsed seaweed with 1 tablespoon of soup soy sauce. Sauté for another 3 minutes.

3. Add 6 cups of water and another ½ tablespoon of soup soy sauce. Cover, and let it come to a boil.

4. Lower heat to medium-low, and keep soup boiling, covered, for another 15 to 20 minutes.

5. Adjust seasoning, adding salt and pepper to taste. Serve with rice and a variety of Korean *banchan* (side dishes).

KID
FRIENDLY
T I P

Use your handy kitchen shears to cut up the seaweed into smaller pieces for younger kids. Add some rice directly into the soup for a quick and easy meal.

NOTE Dried seaweed (*miyeok*) typically made for *miyeok guk* can easily be found in a Korean supermarket. If unsure, you can always ask someone to help guide you to the right section.

ASIAN PANTRY

When it comes to Asian cooking, the right ingredients are key. What follows is a list of the most common staples I use at home, but if you are ever at an Asian market, make sure to experiment and try new things! I am also constantly learning and finding new ingredients that surprise me and help broaden my own cooking journey. All the items I describe here are readily found in regular supermarkets and/or online as well as in Asian markets.

DRIED ANCHOVY

Dried anchovy can be found in Korean markets and is essential for making Korean soup stock (*dashi*). *Dashi* is a very common fish stock that is the base for many Korean soups. Whenever I'm in a pinch, anchovy soup broths save the day because they are quick, easy, and tasty. You will need the larger variety of anchovy, and it has to be gutted first. This sounds a little daunting, but I promise you it's not hard at all! You can seal the anchovy in an airtight bag and store it in your freezer. Having dried anchovy on hand will make weeknight dinners very convenient.

DRIED SEA KELP (DASHIMA)

Dried kelp, also known as *dashima* in Korean and *kombu* in Japanese, is an ingredient that brings out that special umami flavour. You can find dried kelp at Asian markets and most grocery stores. The kelp comes as a full sheet or already cut into small squares. I make sure to have some at all times because it is a key component to making flavourful Asian broths.

FURIKAKE SEASONING

Furikake seasoning may be made up of seaweed, white and black sesame seeds, salt, and kelp powder, among other things, depending on the brand. We like to sprinkle furikake seasoning on our rice bowls, rice balls, noodles, and salads. I like the slight texture and flavour this seasoning brings to our dishes.

LAVER (SEAWEED)

Laver, also known as *gim* in Korean and *nori* in Japanese, is a type of edible dried seaweed that comes packaged in large squares. It can be found in most grocery stores and is used for many things, but you may know it best for making sushi rolls. My kids like to place some rice on top of the *gim* and eat it with Korean side dishes (*banchan*). Seaweed can also be toasted in a pan after brushing some sesame oil on top and sprinkling it with a little salt. Voilà! You have yourself toasted seaweed, which makes a great snack or addition to lunchboxes. You can find *gim* already roasted and salted for your convenience. You can also crush or cut it to add to soups, rice bowls, noodles, and salads as a garnish. The possibilities are endless.

MISO PASTE AND SOYBEAN PASTE (DOENJANG)

I like to keep both pastes in our kitchen as they both bring a unique flavour to the table. Miso paste is great for making miso soup, of course, and also for adding to dressings and marinades. Korean *doenjang* (soybean paste) has a stronger, more intense flavour that adds richness and fullness to Korean stews and dipping sauces. Both pastes are made from fermented soybeans. Whenever I smell or taste *doenjang*, it's an immediate portal to my childhood filled with delicious food memories.

OYSTER SAUCE

Oyster sauce helps bring out that essential umami flavour in Asian cooking and is great for stir-fries and noodle dishes. It's a fundamental part of Chinese cooking, but I also use it for specific Korean dishes. My favourite way to incorporate oyster sauce is in meat and vegetable stir-fries. It just adds that extra flavour and kick.

RED CHILI POWDER (GOCHUGARU) AND HOT PEPPER PASTE (GOCHUJANG)

Because red chili powder and hot pepper paste are staples in Korean cooking, I couldn't leave them out. My daughter can handle a little spice, and I like to add a little bit of both into my Korean cooking. Hot pepper paste is great for sauces, marinating meat, kimchi fried rice, and stews to name a few. It adds a distinct sweet and spicy flavour. You can find ones with different heat levels. I personally cannot live without it!

RICE WINE VINEGAR

Rice wine vinegar is made from fermented rice. Adding just a little brings depth and a subtle sweetness to marinades, sauces, and salads. I always have this on hand for just that!

SESAME OIL

Roasted or toasted sesame oil is derived from sesame seeds and has a strong and delicious nutty flavour. It is used frequently in Korean cooking, and I incorporate it in a lot of my Korean recipes. Because it has a low smoke point, it's best to drizzle near the end of cooking or on top of rice and noodle dishes. I like to use sesame oil in Korean *gimbap* rolls, rice balls, soups, and stews, to name only a few dishes, to create that subtle but fragrant classic Korean flavour.

SESAME SEEDS

Roasted sesame seeds come with many nutritional benefits and can be added to many things. For extra protein, we like to sprinkle some on avocado, toast, rice, noodles, salads, and even some desserts! We always have roasted sesame seeds in our pantry. They are definitely a must-have.

SHORT-GRAINED BROWN OR WHITE RICE

Short-grained rice is the most common rice used in Korean cooking and is the one I use most often. It is stickier and has a chewier consistency than long-grained rice. However, I do like to switch to long-grained rice for certain dishes, depending on what I am cooking. Long-grained rice, such as jasmine rice, is usually lighter and fluffier than short-grained. With Korean rice dishes, it is common to mix grains and beans in as well. You can also add a bit of black rice to your rice mixture, which turns the rice into a beautiful shade of purple.

SOY SAUCE

I like to have soy sauce and soup soy sauce stocked in my pantry at all times. You can opt for low sodium soy sauce as well. It can be found in most Asian grocery stores and goes well with stir-fries, fried rice, noodles, and marinades. Soup soy sauce is lighter in colour than regular soy sauce and is essential for Korean soups and broths. Just a little bit goes a long way. Coconut aminos is a good alternative to soy sauce for people with gluten sensitivities.

GLOSSARY OF KOREAN AND OTHER ASIAN TERMS

TERM	MEANING IN ENGLISH
banchan	side dishes
bap	cooked rice
bulgogi	marinated beef
Chuseok	Korean Thanksgiving
dakdoritang	spicy chicken stew
danmuji	pickled daikon radish
dashi	soup stock
dashima (called kombu in Japanese)	dried kelp
dduk guk	rice cake soup
doenjang	soybean paste
donguerang ddeng (also called wanja-jeon)	Korean beef patties
doshirak	lunchbox
gam	persimmon
gim (called nori in Japanese)	roasted seaweed
gimbap	seaweed rice rolls
gochugaru	Korean red chili flakes or powder
gochujang	Korean hot pepper paste
goguma	Korean sweet potato
guk	soup
guk ganjang	soup soy sauce
gyeran bap	egg rice bowl
gyeran jjim	Korean steamed egg
gyeran mari	rolled Korean-style omelette
japchae	Korean glass noodles
jeon	pancakes
juk	rice porridge
miyeok	dried seaweed
miyeok guk	seaweed soup
omurice (Japanese dish)	omelette and rice
saeng sun jeon	fried fish
soegogi yachae juk	beef and vegetable rice porridge
tteokbokki	rice cakes
yachae gyeran juk	vegetable egg rice porridge

LUNCHBOX SAFETY

By Dani Lebovitz (Kid Food Explorers) and Alicia "Chacha" Miller (The Cardamom), Registered Pediatric Dietitian Nutritionists

ENSURING HEALTHY AND SAFE MEALS ON THE GO

When it comes to packing lunchboxes for our kiddos, we want to provide them with not only delicious and nutritious meals but also ones that are safe to eat. The most important things to remember for lunchbox packing are clean hands and surfaces and keeping food at the proper temperature.

Before packing lunches, make sure to wash your hands with soap and warm water for 20 seconds. Ensure surfaces such as cutting boards, countertops, dishes, and utensils are clean before you get started. Also, be sure to remind your kiddo to wash their hands before eating!

Keep hot foods hot and cold foods cold to minimize the risk of bacterial growth and food-borne illnesses. Invest in insulated lunchboxes, thermoses, and ice packs to keep perishable items safe to eat. Keep cold foods, such as sandwiches, yogurt, and cut fruits and vegetables, at a temperature below 40°F. Keep hot foods, like soups, stews, and casseroles, at a temperature above 140°F. And although it may be tempting to hold on to leftovers that return untouched, it's best to discard any perishable foods, like yogurt, milk, or meat, that have been sitting at the incorrect temperature for an extended period of time.

For more tips on keeping foods safe to eat, check out https://www.foodsafety.gov/.

KEEPING LUNCHES SAFE AND CHOKE-FREE

Food choking hazards are a serious concern when it comes to feeding kids, especially kids under 5. To keep our kids safe, consider age-appropriate foods and textures, avoiding hard or round-shaped foods that pose a higher risk. Be mindful of your child's individual skill level and cut foods into manageable, bite-sized pieces that are easy to chew. Encourage your kiddo to take their time and enjoy each bite, reminding them that meals are not a race. Create a safe environment by staying informed about common choking hazards such as nuts, grapes, hot dogs, popcorn, and chunks of meat or cheese.

For more tips on keeping foods safe to eat, check out https://www.cdc.gov/nutrition/infantandtoddlernutrition/foods-and-drinks/choking-hazards.html.

HERE ARE THE MOST COMMON CHOKING HAZARDS FOR KIDS UNDER 5:

Cherry tomatoes: Cherry tomatoes have a similar size and texture to small balls, making them easy to swallow without proper chewing. It is important to cut them into smaller pieces before serving.

Grapes: Grapes are a common choking hazard due to their small size and smooth texture, making them difficult to chew and swallow for young children.

Hard candies: Hard candies can break into small, sharp pieces if bitten incorrectly, presenting a choking risk. It is advisable to avoid giving hard candies to young children.

Hot dogs: Hot dogs can easily become lodged in a child's throat due to their cylindrical shape and dense texture. It's important to cut them into small, bite-sized pieces before serving.

Marshmallows: The soft and sticky texture of marshmallows can cause them to become lodged in a child's throat. It is best to avoid giving marshmallows to young children or cut them into smaller, more manageable pieces.

Nuts and seeds: Whole nuts and seeds can pose a choking risk, especially for young children who may have difficulty chewing them properly. It is recommended to offer nut butters or finely ground nuts instead.

Peanut butter: While peanut butter itself is not a choking hazard, a large spoonful or a thick layer of peanut butter can be difficult for young children to swallow. It's recommended to spread a thin layer of peanut butter on bread or crackers.

Popcorn: The small, hard kernels of popcorn can get lodged in a child's throat, making it a potential choking hazard. It's best to avoid serving popcorn to children under 5 years old.

Raw carrots and celery: Raw carrots and celery sticks can be difficult for young children to chew and swallow properly, increasing the risk of choking. It is recommended to serve these vegetables thinly sliced or cook them until they are soft.

Special Thanks

I am incredibly grateful to everyone who supported me in the creation of this book.

First and foremost, I want to express my heartfelt thanks to my mom. You have been an immense inspiration, instilling in me a deep love and appreciation for food. Your culinary expertise and your love language of cooking have guided me on my own journey. I aspire to possess the same *son mat* (hand taste) as you when I cook for my own children. Thank you for patiently answering my numerous phone calls, providing details and measurements, and offering your very own "a little bit of this and that" advice.

To my dad, thank you for your never-ending support of all my decisions and endeavours.

To my one and only daughter, Ella, you have been my first muse, and now you're standing beside me in the kitchen, testing my recipes, sharing your insights, and even giving me styling directions. I love you so much, and I couldn't have embarked on this journey without you by my side.

To my son, Chase, thank you for appreciating every dish I make. Your enthusiastic thumbs-up signs, requests for seconds, and constant encouragement mean the world to me. Your beautiful heart and infectious smile will forever be captured within the pages of this book.

My gratitude goes to my husband, Mark, for being my biggest supporter. Thank you for being there through the ups and downs, offering me your time and energy, and always being there to clean up after me. You are not only the best taste-tester but also an incredible dad.

A special thank you goes to my publisher, Maggie Goh, for turning my dream into reality and giving me this incredible opportunity. Your unwavering support, valuable feedback, and belief in me have been instrumental in making this achievement possible. I appreciate every meeting, phone call, email, and guidance. I would also like to extend my gratitude to the entire Plumleaf Press team, including Rebecca Bender and Robin Forsyth, for their brilliance, dedication, creativity, and hard work. Thank you for being an integral part of this journey.

I want to express my appreciation to all my friends and family who generously answered my countless requests and phone calls. Thank you for being my taste-testers, modelling for my cookbook, answering technical, photography, and writing questions, and simply checking in. I am grateful to my cousins, Tina and Charles

Kim, my brother and sister-in-law, Steve and Jeong-hee, and my friends Paula Yoo, David Kang, Kelly Pfeiffer, and the entire Nosh team for their unwavering support. A special thank you to my mother-in-law, Diane, and sister-in-law, Sarah Nicholson, for recipe input and for showing me the joy in cooking together as a family. Thank you to Jennifer Kalynuik for introducing me to my publisher. Thank you to Joan Nguyen and the Bumo parent community, Agnes Hsu, and John Stamos and Caitlin McHugh Stamos for your kind words and insightful reviews. And special thanks to Dani Lebovitz and Chacha Miller for writing an amazing, helpful, informative, and thoughtful foreword. I am grateful to Esme Gardiner, Aila Monahan, and Camila and Wolfie Negin for being incredible models, and to their moms, Candice Watson, Emily Baird, and Sarah Lozoff, for their support and assistance in making it all happen.

Lastly, I want to express my deepest gratitude to my Food Kids Love community. Without your support, none of this would have been possible. Thank you for allowing me to be a part of your lives.

Thank you all from the bottom of my heart.

Jane

About Jane Kim Nicholson

Jane Kim Nicholson is a blogger, food and lifestyle photographer, and the writer and creator of Food Kids Love, a non-judgmental, accessible space that provides everyday inspiration for kid-friendly snacks, lunchboxes, and meals.

Jane was born and raised in Canada, where she obtained a double honours bachelor of arts degree in English and Mass Communications. Several of her past recipes and lunchboxes have been mentioned in media outlets, including BuzzFeed, Greatist, and The Insider, including a small feature in the cookbook *The Simple Lunchbox*, by Jacqueline Linder, founder of LunchBots.

As a daughter of Korean immigrant parents, Jane has built up fond memories and a love of food and cooking from helping in her parents' restaurants and cafes growing up. Driven by her heritage, she is dedicated to using food as a way to appreciate and embrace the diversity of cultures, aiming to make a positive impact.

Jane currently resides in Los Angeles, California, with her husband, two kids, and a little rescue dog named Bear.

As a busy mom of two, Jane knows a thing or two about simple and healthy meals that even the pickiest eaters will love. If you want to see more of her tips and tricks, follow her on Instagram, TikTok, and Pinterest or check out her website, foodkidslove.com.

 INSTAGRAM
 TIKTOK
 PINTEREST
 WEBSITE

INDEX

IMAGE CREDITS

Endpaper: squigly lines—Polina Tomtosova/Shutterstock.com; 52: chia seeds—Neosiam/Getty Images; [cinnamon, banana, milk, pineapple] Billion Photos/Canva Pro; mango—Ancelin/pixabay; [avocado, spinach, peanut butter] Layer-Lab/Canva Pro; Hemp Hearts—MichellePatrickPhotographyLLC from Getty Images; blueberries—Elena Photo/Canva Pro; cinnamon—bdspnimage/Canva Pro; chia seeds—krimkate/Canva Pro; 53: dragon fruit—Anna Kucherova/Canva Pro; mango—Ancelin/pixabay; Greek yogurt—Billion Photos/Canva Pro; mint leaves—Anna Kucherova/Canva Pro; pistachio—Layer-Lab/Canva Pro; 80: [almonds, raspberry]—Billion Photos/Canva Pro; 137: [balloons—Infinity design; shamrocks—Miceking; pumpkins—Barmaleeva; snowflakes—ace03] Shutterstock.com; 165: Christmas ornament—leekris/Getty Images; 176: dashima—4kodiak/Getty Images Signature; anchovies—vvoennyy/Envato Elements; furikake seasoning—bhofack2/Envato Elements; 177: miso paste: charlotteLake/Envato Elements; hot pepper paste—Virginia Garcia/Shutterstock.com; laver— ikadapurhangus/Envato Elements 178: rice—Artem_ka/Envato Elements; sesame oil and seeds—Africa images/Canva Pro; 180: yellow tablecloth—merc67/Getty Images; 181: carrots and celery—Taden/Getty Images; cherry tomatoes—Layer-Lab/Canva Pro; [grapes. hard candy, nuts] Billion Photos/Canva Pro; hotdogs—xamtiw/Envato Elements; popcorn—Darya Fedorova/Canva Pro